Ruling AND Reigning ON THE Throne OF David

John Eckhardt

Crusaders Ministries
Chicago, Illinois

Unless otherwise indicated, all scriptural quotations are from the
King James Version of the Bible © 1982 by Thomas Nelson, Inc.

The Amplified Bible © 1965 by the Zondervan Publishing House.

The Bible: An American Translation by J. M. Powis Smith and Edgar J. Goodspeed.
© 1935 by the University of Chicago

Praise-Songs of Israel: A Rendering of the Book of Psalms by John *DeWitt*.

The Psalms for Today: A New translation From the Hebrew Into Current English by
R. K. *Harrison* © 1961 by the Zondervan Publishing House.

The Jerusalem Bible © 1966 by the Darton, Longman, and Todd, Ltd. and Doubleday and Company, Inc.

The Holy Bible: A Translation From the Latin Vulgate in the Light of the Hebrew and Greek Originals by Monsignor Ronald *Knox*. © 1954 by Sheed and Ward, Inc., New York, with the permission of His Eminence, the Cardinal Archbishop of westminster and Burns and Oates, Ltd.

A New Translation of the Bible © 1954 by James *Moffatt*. Used by permission of Harper and Row, Inc and Hodder and Stoughton, Ltd.

The New American Standard Bible of the Bible © 1960, 1962, 1963 by The Lockman Foundation.

The New Berkeley Version in Modern English © 1945, 1959, 1969 by the Zondervan Publishing House.

The New English Bible © 1961, 1970 by The Delegates of the Oxford University Press and The Syndics of the Cambridge University Press.

The Revised Standard Version of the Bible © 1946, 1952, by the Division of Christian Education of the National Council of the Christ in the U.S.A.

A Translation of the Old Testament scriptures From the Original Hebrew by Helen *Spurrel*.

The Living Bible: Paraphrased by Kenneth *Taylor* © 1971 by Tyndale House Publishers.

Ruling and Reigning on the Throne of David
Published by:
Crusaders Ministries
6150 West North Avenue
Chicago, IL 60639
ISBN 1-883927-16-1

Copyright © 2001 by John Eckhardt
All rights reserved.
Reproduction of text in whole or in part without the express written consent by the author is not permitted and is unlawful according to the 1976 United States Copyright Act.

Cover design and book production by:
DB & Associates Design Group, Inc.
dba Double Blessing Productions
P.O. Box 52756, Tulsa, OK 74152
www.doubleblessing.com
Cover illustration is protected by the 1976 United States Copyright Act.
Copyright © 2001 by DB & Associates Design Group, Inc.

Editorial Consultant: Debra Marshall

Printed in the United States of America.

Contents

Acknowledgements

Introduction

1. The Davidic Generation 1
2. The Spirit of David 5
3. A Generation That Worships Like David 9
4. A Covenant Relationship Generation 19
5. Prosperity on David's Throne 29
6. Wisdom and Revelation on David's Throne 39
7. Great Favor on David's Throne 47
8. A Praying and Prophectic Generation 53
9. Returning the Ark of God 61
10. A Generation That Recovers All 65
11. A Generation That Wars Like David 77
12. A Kingdom Dominion Generation 89
13. Excellence and Order on David's Throne 95
14. Ruling and Reigning with Jesus on
    the Throne of David 111

Acknowledgements

Special thanks and gratitude to the following members of our local church who sowed seed towards the publication of this end-time message.

1. Joe W. Beal
2. Priscilla Benjamin
3. Donald Brown
4. Linda L. Chaney
5. Jacque Cook
6. Amber D. Wright-Estes
7. Dennis and Avis Ganter
8. Karen N. Guice
9. Jewel Harris
10. Gail Jackson
11. Robin Johnson
12. Michelle McClain
13. Wayne McClelland
14. Angeleka Mendler
15. Eugene and Jacqueline Record
16. Marlinda M. House-Rhodes
17. Anna M. Page-Roberts
18. Velita A. Sanders
19. Debra A. Sanders
20. Debra A. Seaton, ESQ.
21. Deborah A. Simmons
22. Sharol Unger-Stewart
23. Dudley Throupe
24. Dorothy Thurman
25. Suberina Tidwell

King David's throne is prophetic for the Church.

Victories won by King David represent your victories in Christ.

King David's anointing was passed on to his men who were able to do exploits.

Jesus Christ, our King David, passes His anointing on to you, and you too can do exploits.

King Solomon is an extension of David's throne. The true wisdom is found in Jesus. This is the believer's inheritance. Claim your wisdom by faith just as you do your healing.

There was much wealth on David's throne. This was also manifested in Solomon's kingdom. Jesus Christ (our David) gives us all things to enjoy. All the money you will ever need for your ministry on earth is provided in Jesus.

King David was famous. Jesus was famous. Jesus in you is famous. Claim this fame for the body of Christ. Claim this fame for your own ministry, and then hold your confession. Work it out in your life.

King David's throne was one of joy as he danced before the Lord. Jesus was anointed with joy above his fellows. You are on a joy throne.

Form a picture in your mind of a throne with you sitting there with Jesus. Let this picture of your throne bring you through your problems.

—Bob Buess,
<u>King David and I</u>

Introduction

This is an apostolic and prophetic generation. The spirit of David is coming back to the Church. Jesus is the Greater David. We are the seed of David through Christ. God is rebuilding the Tabernacle of David which is fallen down. Davidic praise and worship is returning to the Church. The psalmists, minstrels, and dancers are coming forth. The prophets are arising in the Church. The ark is being restored to the Church.

This is a warfare generation. We are fighting like king David through Jesus Christ. We are receiving an anointing to war and overcome the enemy. David's victories are prophetic types of our victories. This is an exciting time to be alive. We are accessing the throne of David through Jesus Christ. We are tapping into this vein and the blessings that accompany it. David's throne is being established in this generation through the Church.

Chapter 1
The Davidic Generation

The Throne of David

I believe this revelation of the throne of David will change your life, your ministry, your business, and everything that concerns you. Get ready to enter into a new level of dominion and authority. Rarely have I ever been so excited about writing a book as with this one. The truths in this book will set you free from any mentality that is not conducive to your advancement and progress. I pray that the eyes of your understanding will be opened to the truths in this book. You will become a part of this end-time Davidic generation of believers that God is raising up in the earth.

I have had these truths in my spirit for over ten years. This is the first time I am putting them in print. There is another realm that the Lord is bringing the Church into. It is a realm of apostolic power, dominion, and authority. This is the dawning of a new day for the Church.

The throne of David is a prophetic picture of the rule of Christ through His church. The kings who sat upon the throne of David are also prophetic types of the end-time Church. The godly kings who ruled and reigned in Israel are types of the end-time victorious Church that is arising in the earth. Their dominion, prosperity, wisdom, and greatness are all pictures of God's will for His church today.

The Throne of David Still Exists Today

He shall build me an house, and I will stablish his throne forever.

I will be his father, and he shall be my son: and I will not take my mercy away from him, as I took it from him that was before thee:

But I will settle him in mine house and in my kingdom for ever: and his throne shall be established for evermore.

According to all these words, and according to all this vision, so did Nathan speak unto David.

1 Chronicles 17:12-15

Of all the blessings that God bestowed upon King David, perhaps the greatest blessing was God's promise to establish his house throughout all generations. God promised not to take away His mercy from David like He did from Saul. God promised to establish David's throne FOREVER. This of course is fulfilled in Jesus Christ, who is the Seed of David. Although many of David's descendants sinned, God's mercy remained upon the house of David. David, like any king, was concerned about his throne. God assured him through the prophet Nathan that his throne would last forever.

And David the king came and sat before the LORD, and said, Who am I, O LORD God, and what is mine house, that thou hast brought me hitherto?

And yet this is a small thing in thine eyes, O God; for thou hast also spoken of thy servants house for a great while to come, and hast regarded me according to the estate of a man of high degree, O LORD God.

> What can David speak more to thee for the honor of thy servant? for thou knowest thy servant.
>
> O LORD, for thy servants sake, and according to thine own heart, hast thou done all this greatness, in making known all these great things...
>
> Therefore now, LORD, let the thing that thou hast spoken concerning thy servant and concerning his house be established for ever, and do as thou hast said.
>
> Let it even be established, that thy name may be magnified for ever, saying, The LORD of hosts is the God of Israel: and let the house of David thy servant be established before thee.
>
> 1 Chronicles 17:16-19,23-24

David received the word and praised God for His favor and mercy. David's throne is a great throne. David was the greatest of Israel's kings. There is more concerning his life and reign than any other king in the Bible. Jesus is the Greater David. The Church is brought into David's blessing through Christ. We rule and reign upon David's throne with Jesus Christ. The purpose of this throne is that the NAME OF THE LORD BE MAGNIFIED FOREVER. As we rule from this throne, the name of the Lord is magnified.

> Now therefore let it please thee to bless the house of thy servant, that it might be before thee for ever: for thou blessest, O LORD, and it shall be blessed for ever.
>
> 1 Chronicles 17:27

David's house is BLESSED forever. The throne of David is BLESSED forever. There are certain blessings attached to this throne. Every king that sat upon this throne had access to this blessing. It was the most blessed throne to sit upon in all the earth because it was blessed by God. As we sit upon this throne with Jesus, we also have access to these blessings which include anointing, favor, mercy, fame, wealth, victory, great deliverance, greatness, the prophetic ministry, praise, worship, and the glory of God. *Blessed* means marked by God's favor. It also means saved, redeemed, glorified, exalted, rewarded, resurrected, and holy. *Blessing* means benefit, good, advantage, good fortune, and miracle. Blessings bring joy and happiness.

Once have I sworn by my holiness that I will not lie unto David.

His seed shall endure for ever, and his THRONE as the sun before me.

It shall be established for ever as the moon, and as a faithful witness in heaven. Selah.
Psalm 89:35-37

We are the seed of David through Jesus Christ. The Church shall endure forever. It is eternal. It cannot be conquered or destroyed. The Church has inherited the throne of David. *David was a man of authority and dominion.* He was anointed to rule and reign. He is a type of the apostolic church.

He shall be great, and shall be called the Son of the Highest; and the Lord God shall give unto him the THRONE OF HIS FATHER DAVID.
Luke 1:32

Jesus inherited the throne of his father David. Jesus is the true David of prophecy. Jesus sits upon the throne of David. As believers we reign with Christ from David's throne. We are joint heirs with Christ.

Throughout the Old Testament, David's throne is spoken of in a prophetic way. Jesus is the fulfillment of that prophecy. Everything good that happened on David's throne was prophetic of the reign of Jesus through the Church. (Bob Buess)

Chapter 2
The Spirit of David

The Key of David

The key of David is an ancient key. It is a master key that opens all doors. *Nothing is shut to them who have the key of David.* It is the key of the king. Everything in the Kingdom is opened with this key.

> **And the key of the house of David will I lay upon his shoulder; so he shall open, and none shall shut; and he shall shut, and none shall open.**
> **Isaiah 22:22**

> **And to the angel of the church in Philadelphia write; These things saith he that is holy, he that is true, he that hath the key of David, he that openeth, and no man shutetth; and shutteth, and no man openeth.**
>
> **I know thy works: behold, I have set before thee an open door, and no man can shut it: for thou hast a little strength, and hast kept my word, and hast not denied my name.**
> **Revelation 3:7,8**

God is setting before you an open door. No man can shut what is being opened unto you. Jesus now has the key of David. You are connected to Him and this key through salvation. Begin to use the key of David. Begin to use the authority you have to open doors.

This is the authority to bind and loose. We have the key of David to open and close doors. This is the day of opened and closed doors. Doors to the nations are opened to us as we sit upon the throne of David. Financial doors are opened unto us. These are great and effectual doors (1 Corinthians 16:9).

Doors represent opportunity. The Knox translation says, "a great opportunity lies open to me." Doors are being opened over cities, regions, and nations. *This is the day of the open door.* See doors being opened to you as you exercise your authority using the key of David. Doors that were previously closed will now be opened unto you. New opportunities for ministry and business will come open suddenly.

Though he had commanded the clouds from above, and opened the doors of heaven,   **Psalm 78:23**

The LORD sitteth upon the flood;...
   Psalm 29:10

...if I will not open you the windows of heaven, and pour out a blessing, that there shall not be room enough to receive it.   **Malachi 3:10**

The Jerusalem translation says, "the floodgates of heaven." Get ready for the floods. *Flood* means a deluge. There is a deluge of blessing coming your way because of the gates of heaven being opened. *God is upon this flood.* A flood is an overflow. A flood goes beyond the boundaries of the river. The boundaries cannot contain the flood. You will not have enough room to receive the blessings that come by using the key of David.

Keys provide entry and access. We have access to great blessing while we sit on the throne of David. We have access to the mysteries of God. We have access to the prophetic ministry. We have access to wealth and prosperity. We have access to fame and greatness. We have access to wisdom and revelation. This is because we have the key of David. The Church is beginning to use this key and open things that have been previously shut to her, the Bride of Christ. We are also using this key to bind up the works of the devil.

> And he said unto him, Verily, verily, I say unto you, Hereafter ye shall see heaven open, and the angels ascending and descending upon the Son of man.
> John 1:51

The key of David causes heaven to be opened over your life. This includes angelic activity. Angels have been sent forth to minister for those who are the heirs of salvation. Angels help us break through obstacles and opposition. There is an angelic army waiting to assist you. You are not alone on David's throne. Heaven is opened over your life to provide all you need to rule and reign in this life.

> And a certain woman named Lydia, a seller of purple, of the city of Thyatira, which worshipped God, heard us: whose heart the Lord opened,...
> Acts 16:14

This key opens the hearts of men. People will begin to open their hearts to you as you minister to them. People will begin to open their hearts to the message God has given you. Multitudes are opening their hearts to salvation. This is the result of the end-time Church using the key of David.

> AND they said one to another, Did not our heart burn within us, while he talked with us by the way, and while he opened to us the scriptures?
> Luke 24:32

The Word of God will open to us with the key of David. Our eyes are being opened to hidden things. We are seeing what we never saw before. New revelation and insight is yours as you sit upon the throne of David.

It is given unto us to know the mysteries of the Kingdom. Begin to see the Word of God open up to you as you study and read it. The words will begin to leap off the pages. It will come alive to you as you sit on the throne of David.

We open up new places in the spirit with the key of David. As a pioneer you open the way for others to follow. We open places in the spirit for men to enter in. We open places in the spirit where men have never been. *This is the day of openings.* Receive the key of David by faith and begin to use it by faith.

A believer had a vision of old, rusty locks on old gates in a city. These locks had not been opened for centuries. No one had the key. But we will open the old locks. The key of David is our ancient key. We are recovering this ancient key and using it in our generation. It takes the right key to open certain locks. Without the right key, we have no access. The key of David is a master key. It opens all the locks. There is nothing that you will not be able to access as you sit upon the throne of David.

And one of the elders saith unto me, Weep not: behold, the Lion of the tribe of Juda the Root of David, hath prevailed to open the book, and to loose the seven seals thereof.
Revelation 5:5

Jesus has prevailed to open the book and loose the seals. He is the Root of David. He has the key of David. This is the day of openings.

Chapter 3
A Generation That Worships Like David

The Sure Mercies of David

And as concerning that he raised him from the dead, now no more to return to corruption, he said on this wise, I will give you the SURE MERCIES OF DAVID.

Wherefore he saith also in another psalm, Thou shalt not suffer thine Holy One to see corruption.

Acts 13:34,35

But God, who is rich in mercy, for his great love wherewith he loved us,

Even when we were dead in sins, hath quickened us together with Christ, (by grace are ye saved;)

And hath raised us up together, and made us sit together in heavenly places in Christ Jesus:

Ephesians 2:4-6

The apostles connected the sure mercies of David with the resurrection. We were dead in sins. We have been quickened (made alive) in Christ and raised with Him. We are partakers of the sure mercies of David. We are now sitting together in heavenly places in Christ Jesus. There is no greater mercy than being dead in sin and brought back to life in Christ Jesus.

We are joint heirs with Jesus Christ. We also inherit the *sure mercies* of David. Remember, David is a type of an end-time apostolic church. Apostolic churches will walk in the sure mercies of David.

The Revised Standard Version says, *"I will give unto you the holy and sure blessings of David."* The New English Bible says, *"I will give unto you, the blessings promised to David, holy and pure."*

There are certain blessings associated with David. There are certain promises to David. These mercies and promises can be found in Psalm 89. They are SURE. This means they are stedfast and we can depend upon them. They cannot be revoked. God has sworn to have mercy upon David and his seed. The saints need to have a revelation of this and walk in it by faith. There is great mercy released upon the Church through Jesus Christ. Begin to see yourself living under this mercy.

And that the Gentiles might glorify God for his mercy; as it is written, For this cause I will confess to thee among the Gentiles, and sing unto thy name.

And again he saith, Rejoice, ye Gentiles, with his people.

And again, Praise the Lord, all ye Gentiles; and laud him, all ye people.

Romans 15:9-11

We praise God for this mercy. Mercy causes us to rejoice. The Gentiles are partakers of the mercy of God. All the nations are to sing His praise. We praise the Lord as we sit on the throne of David.

There are many blessings connected to God's mercy. Mercy is more than forgiveness of sins. It is the compassion and love of God. David experienced this and so can we. David was highly favored and loved by God in spite of his weaknesses and shortcomings. He was forgiven and blessed. He was raised to a position of greatness because of God's mercy. This was not so with Saul. He was removed from his throne because of his transgression. God will have mercy upon whom He wills *(Romans 9:15)*. God has chosen to place His mercy upon David's house and this includes the Church.

I WILL sing of the mercies of the LORD forever: with my mouth will I make known thy faithfulness to all generations.

Psalm 89:1

David sang of God's mercy. He understood the blessing that mercy had upon his life. He testifies of God's mercy to all generations. There are people in every generation that will experience God's mercy. They are chosen and favored by God. *You must see yourself chosen and highly favored by God.*

The American Standard Version translation says, *"I will sing of the lovingkindness of Jehovah forever."* Mercy is lovingkindness. God's love and kindness rested upon David and his seed. See yourself walking under God's love and kindness. You are connected to the throne of David through Jesus Christ.

The Psalmist speaks of God's faithfulness to all generations. Davidic churches will affect generations. They make known God's faithfulness to all generations. God is faithful to David. He is faithful to His church. He will not violate this covenant. It is a sure covenant. These mercies are sure. This means you can depend on them. Mercies also mean favor. God has favors for David. Remember we sit on David's throne through Jesus Christ. All of the promises of God are fulfilled in Jesus.

For I have said, Mercy shall be built up forever: thy faithfulness shalt thou establish in the very heavens.

Psalm 89:2

Other translations use the word KINDNESS. God is kind unto David. This kindness reaches to the Church. David had a revelation of God's kindness and faithfulness.

I have made a covenant with my chosen, I have sworn unto David my servant.
                                             Psalm 89:3

David was chosen. God established His covenant with David. David had a special covenant with God. There are certain promises and blessings that go with this covenant. The Church is now the beneficiary of this covenant through Jesus Christ. We need to walk in this covenant and receive the blessings associated with it.

Thy seed will I establish for ever, and build up thy throne to all generations. Selah.
                                             Psalm 89:4

God's promise to David is for all generations. Who are the covenant people of this generation? I believe they are the believers who are walking in the spirit of David. This is an apostolic and prophetic spirit. God promised to build up David's throne. A throne is a place of dominion. It is a place of authority. Apostolic churches are churches of dominion and authority. They minister from the throne. They rule and reign with Jesus Christ. Allow these truths to get into your spirit. Know that God is building up the throne of David today. He is building His church.

And the heavens shall praise thy wonders, O LORD: thy faithfulness also in the congregation of the saints.
                                             Psalm 89:5

The Amplified version says, *"Let heaven (the angels) praise Your wonders, O Lord."*

Angels in heaven are connected to David's throne. They praise God for His wonders. We will see wonders through David's throne. Apostolic churches will know the ministry of angels. We are linked to them in the spirit. As we praise God for His mercy and wonders on the earth, they praise God in the heavens.

For who in the heaven can be compared unto the LORD? who among the sons of the mighty can be likened unto the LORD? **Psalm 89:6**

Those who walk in the covenant of David have a revelation of God's greatness.

The house of David knows the greatness of God. David's house (the Church) is great, because our God is great. God is raising up a great Church and a great people. We are great because we are connected with Jesus.

God is greatly to be feared in the assembly of the saints, and to be had in reverence of all them that are about him. **Psalm 89:7**

Davidic churches will be known for the fear of the Lord. They will have a holy reverence for God. This can be seen in our lifestyles and in our worship

O LORD God of hosts, who is a strong LORD like unto thee? Or to thy faithfulness round about thee? **Psalm 89:8**

Davidic churches have a revelation of the strength of God and the faithfulness of God. David knew the strength of God, and so can we. God is raising up a strong church and a strong people. We are seeing strong prayer, strong preaching, strong meat of the Word, strong praise and worship. The strength of God is flowing into the Church. Strong apostles and prophets are continually being raised up.

Thou rulest the raging of the sea: when the waves thereof arise, thou stillest them. **Psalm 89:9**

This is a picture of God's rule. God rules through David. The throne of David is a place of God's rule through His church. God rules the tumultuous sea. The sea represents the nations. Davidic people rule the nations from David's throne.

Thou hast broken Rahab in pieces, as one that is slain; thou hast scattered thine enemies with thy strong arm.
Psalm 89:10

Rahab is a spirit of pride. It represents arrogance, rebellion, and haughtiness. God breaks the pride of man through David's throne. He scatters the spirits of pride with His strong arm. He breaks the kingdoms of pride through His Davidic people. We are seeing strongholds of pride come down. Arrogant kingdoms are subject to us who sit on David's throne.

The heavens are thine, the earth also is thine: as for the world and the fullness thereof, thou hast founded them.
Psalm 89:11

This verse gives a picture of God's dominion. Davidic churches operate in God's dominion. They exercise authority in the heavens, the earth, and the world. We are attacking ruling spirits in the heavens. We are casting out demons on the earth. We have a vision for the nations.

The north and the south thou hast created them: Tabor and Hermon shall rejoice in thy name.
Psalm 89:12

Remember this is prophetic terminology. Davidic people will rule the north and the south. *Tabor* means broken region. Davidic churches are called to broken regions. We are called to broken nations and cities. They all come under the dominion of God. *Hermon* means abrupt. It is taken from the word meaning snub-nosed.

It means that which is cut off. We will rule over these regions from David's throne.

Thou hast a mighty arm: strong is thy hand, and high is thy right hand.

Psalm 89:13

The Harrison translation says, "You are possessed with formidable strength: Your activity is vigorous, Your resources immense." Davidic people have a revelation of the strength of God. God is active in the earth. His resources are immense.

Justice and judgment are the habitation of thy throne: mercy and truth shall go before thy face.

Psalm 89:14

Justice and judgment are released from David's throne. Mercy and truth are connected to David's throne.

We are called to execute God's judgment and justice upon the earth. We are called to release God's mercy and truth.

Blessed is the people that know the joyful sound: they shall walk, O Lord, in the light of thy countenance.

Psalm 89:15

Davidic people are people of joy. There is joy on David's throne. They are people of strength. The joy of the Lord is our strength. They walk in the light of God's countenance. The Harrison translation says, *"who go about radiant with Your presence."* The Spurrel translation says, *"They shall proceed under the smile of thy face, O Jehovah."* We are to rule and reign with joy. There is an anointing of joy. Jesus is anointed with the oil of gladness. We are not to reign in sorrow. Reigning with Jesus is not a burden but a joy.

> **For the Kingdom of God is not meat and drink; but righteousness, and peace, and joy in the Holy Ghost.**
> **Romans 14:17**

> **In thy name shall they rejoice all the day: and in thy righteousness shall they be exalted.**
> **Psalm 89:16**

Davidic people rejoice in the Lord and boast in His righteousness. There is much rejoicing in the house of David. There is dancing and celebration. This is Davidic praise and worship. It is not somber and sad, but of joy and gladness. We walk in the righteousness of Christ. David's tabernacle was a type of the New Testament church. There was much rejoicing in this tabernacle. It was different from the tabernacle of Moses. We are not bound by legalism, but set free to enjoy the glorious liberty of the Holy Spirit.

> **For thou art the glory of their strength: and in thy favour our horn shall be exalted.**
> **Psalm 89:17**

This is a prophetic word for the Church. We are exalted because of God's favor. There is much favor on David's throne. There are many blessings that are connected to the favor of God. David was favored by God. Jesus increased in favor with God and man. The early Church walked in God's favor. We are accessing the throne of David and tapping into supernatural favor.

> **For the LORD is our defence; and the Holy One of Israel is our king.**
> **Psalm 89:18**

Our defense is of God. David had many enemies. God was his defense. The Church's enemies are many, but God is our defense. There are many enemies to the throne of David. Demons hate the rule of God through the Church. They resist and oppose it, but our protection is of God. We need not fear the enemy. Supernatural protection is a part of David's covenant.

Then thou spakest in vision to thy holy one, and saidst, I have laid help upon one that is mighty; I have exalted one chosen out of the people.
Psalm 89:19

Other translations speak of a diadem upon David's head. The crown is a symbol of authority. We have inherited the crown of David.

I have found David my servant; with my holy oil I have anointed him.
Psalm 89:20

Davidic people are anointed. There is a Davidic anointing being released upon the Church. We walk in David's blessing because we carry this anointing. It is an end-time apostolic anointing. David is a type of the apostolic ministry. We must be anointed to sit upon David's throne.

With whom my hand shall be established: mine arm also shall strengthen him.
Psalm 89:21

The Harrison translation says, *"My power will sustain him."* The Taylor translation says, *"I will steady him and make him strong."* We are made strong by the Lord. This is a part of David's blessings.

The enemy shall not exact upon him; nor the son of wickedness afflict him.
Psalm 89:22

This is one of the greatest blessings of David. The PBV version says, *"The enemy shall not be able to do him violence; the son of wickedness shall not hurt him."* The Revised Standard Version says, *"The enemy shall not outwit him, the wicked shall not humble him."* The enemy cannot rule over David. Our enemies cannot subdue us.

And I will beat down his foes before his face, and plague them that hate him.
Psalm 89:23

Our enemies are beaten down when we operate from David's throne.

But my faithfulness and my mercy shall be with him: in my name shall his horn be exalted.
Psalm 89:24

God is loyal to David. Throughout this Psalm, we hear references to David's faithfulness. The Knox translation says, *"but my favour he shall rise to preeminence."* The Harrison translation says, *"his prestige shall increase."* The Moffat translation says, *"I will lift him high in honour."*

I will set his hand also in the sea, and his right hand in the rivers.
Psalm 89:25

David's dominion was from the Mediterranean sea to the river Euphrates. God establishes us in our boundaries. Our line goes throughout the earth *(Psalm 19:4).*

Chapter 4
A Covenant Relationship Generation

He shall cry unto me, Thou art my father, my God, and the rock of my salvation.   **Psalm 89:26**

David tapped into the Fatherhood of God. He operated as a son. This is a picture of Jesus the Son of God. This is sonship. Sons receive the inheritance.

Also I will make him my firstborn, higher than the kings of the earth.   Psalm 89:27

Jesus is the firstborn. He is the Seed of David. We partake of the firstborn blessing by being in Christ. Our position is higher than the kings of the earth. We operate in a higher realm of authority. Our authority is greater than natural powers and political authority.

My mercy will I keep for him for evermore, and my covenant shall stand fast with him.   Psalm 89:28

God's covenant is sure. It is everlasting. It goes from generation to generation. There are always those who walk in it. There is always a group that receives these blessings. Each godly king in the line of David benefited from this covenant. Solomon, Jehoshaphat, Asa, Hezekiah, Uzziah, and Josiah all benefited from this covenant. There are churches today that will walk in this covenant. There are believers today who will walk in this covenant.

> **His seed also will I make to endure for ever, and his throne as the days of heaven.**
> **Psalm 89:29**

Jesus is the seed of David. We are His seed because we are in Christ. David's throne endures to all generations. This is a dynasty.

Faith and Obedience To Reign on David's Throne

> **Therefore now, LORD, let the thing that thou hast spoken concerning thy servant and concerning his house be established for ever, and do as thou hast said.**
> **1 Chronicles 17:23**

> **...of David also, and Samuel, and of the prophets:**

> **Who through faith subdued kingdoms, wrought righteousness, OBTAINED PROMISES, stopped the mouth of lions.**
> **Hebrews 11:32,33**

It takes faith and obedience to rule and reign on David's throne. David received the word of the prophet concerning his house. We must rise up in faith and take our place on the throne of David. David was a man of faith. He is mentioned in the *Faith* Hall of Fame. Through faith we obtain God's promises.

...Faith cometh by hearing... (Romans 10:17). As you hear this message, allow faith to arise in your heart, to rule and reign on the throne of David. We can ask God to do as He has said. If He spake it, He will bring it to pass. We are a generation that will rise up and embrace the promises of God to the seed of David. We will walk

in dominion and authority by faith. We will rule and reign with Jesus Christ by faith.

> ...Behold to obey is better than sacrifice, and to hearken than the fat of rams.
>
> For rebellion is as the sin of witchcraft, and stubbornness is as iniquity and idolatry.
>
> 1 Samuel 15:22,23

> I have found David the son of Jesse, a man after mine own heart, which shall fulfill all my will,
>
> Of this man's seed hath God according to his promise raised unto Israel a Saviour, Jesus.
>
> Acts 13:22,23

Saul lost his throne because of disobedience. God looked for another king and found David. David was obedient to do the will of God. This is the testimony of David (...*which shall fulfill all my will;...*). Obedience is necessary to rule and reign on the throne of David. The kings who were obedient to the Law were blessed. Those who disobeyed had much trouble and vexation during their reigns. Rebellion will hinder us from ruling on the throne of David.

> If his children forsake my law, and walk not in my judgments;
>
> If they break my statutes, and keep not my commandments;
>
> Then will I visit their transgression with the rod, and their iniquity with stripes.
>
> Nevertheless my lovingkindness will I not utterly take from him, nor suffer my faithfulness to fail.
>
> Psalm 89:30-33

Chastisement is a part of David's covenant. Disobedience robs us of our ability to rule and reign. Saul was rejected for his disobedience. God searched for another king and found David. God is still searching for a people that will fulfill His will. Jesus was obedient to the will of his Father. He is the Perfect David. He now sits on the throne of David. We rule and reign with Him through our faith and obedience.

Anointed To Sit on David's Throne

> **Then Samuel took the horn of oil, and anointed him in the midst of his brethren: and the Spirit of the LORD came upon David from that day forward....**
>
> **1 Samuel 16:13**
>
> **So the elders of Israel came to the king to Hebron; and king David made a league with them in Hebron before the LORD: and they anointed David king over Israel.**
>
> **DAVID was thirty years old when he began to reign, and he reigned forty years.**
>
> **2 Samuel 5:3,4**

David is a type of Jesus. He was thirty when he began to reign. Jesus was thirty when he began his ministry. David was anointed. Jesus is the Christ which means ANOINTED ONE. We are partakers of this anointing. You must be anointed to sit on David's throne. All of the descendants of David who sat on his throne were anointed.

> **And Zadok the priest took a horn of oil out of the tabernacle, and anointed Solomon. And they blew the trumpet; and all the people said, God save king Solomon.**
>
> **1 Kings 1:39**

This anointing goes from generation to generation. Solomon was anointed as the next king. Jesus is anointed as the King of kings. He sits on the throne of his father David. We are anointed with Christ. We also sit upon the throne of David in our generation.

Great deliverance giveth he to his king; and sheweth mercy to his ANOINTED, to David, and to his seed for evermore.
Psalm 18:50

There are certain responsibilities and blessing that come with being anointed. God shows great mercy to His anointed. You will see great victories as a result of the anointing. The Revised Standard Version says, *"Great triumphs."* Other translations say, *"glorious conquests."*

Now I know that the LORD saveth his ANOINTED; he will hear from his holy heaven with the saving strength of his right hand.
Psalm 20:6

The Moffat translation says, *"Now am I sure the Eternal grants victory to his chosen king."* David knew what it meant to be anointed. He understood the blessing of being anointed. God will answer the prayers of His anointed. Salvation and deliverance comes from being anointed. See yourself partaking of the anointing of Jesus. Christ means anointed. We are partakers of the Christ anointing. We are connected to Jesus Christ (The Anointed One). This is a part of being a Christian. We have been anointed to sit on the throne and rule and reign with Jesus Christ.

...thou anointest my head with oil; my cup runneth over.
Psalm 23:5

The Harrison translation says, *"my fortunes prosper greatly."* The Taylor translation says, *"blessings overflow."* Abundance and overflow belong to you because of the anointing. Your life will overflow to bless others. God gives us more than enough. We are blessed, and God has made us a blessing. See yourself overflowing with blessings as you sit upon the throne of David.

The LORD is their strength, and he is the saving strength of his ANOINTED.
Psalm 28:8

This was the key to David's great strength. It was the key to the ministry of Jesus. The Spirit of God came upon David from the moment he was anointed. He was anointed for battle. We are anointed with the strength of God. Begin to see yourself strong because of the anointing.

O LORD God of hosts, hear my prayer: give ear, O God of Jacob. Selah.

Behold, O God our shield, and look upon the face of thine anointed.
Psalm 84:8,9

The Knox translation says, *"look favorably upon the face of thine anointed."* We can pray and ask for God's favor because of the anointing. You have a special position with God because of the anointing. You are not like everyone else. You are separated for God's purposes through the anointing. God hears your prayers.

Your prayers have a special place before God.

But my horn shalt thou exalt like the horn of a unicorn: I shall be anointed with fresh oil.
Psalm 92:10

There is a fresh anointing being released upon the Church. It is a new thing. We are receiving a fresh apostolic and prophetic anointing for this hour. The Harrison translation says, *"But you have promoted me, so that I am like a powerful buffalo."* We have the strength of a wild ox because of the anointing. See yourself being promoted on the throne of David.

> There will I make the horn of David to bud: I have ordained a lamp for mine anointed.
>
> Psalm 132:17

God has prepared a lamp for His anointed. A lamp represents authority. We have light and revelation as we sit on the throne of David. A lamp causes us to shine. We shine in the darkness. People are attracted to this lamp. We carry the light and the glory of God.

> Thus saith the Lord to his ANOINTED, to Cyrus, whose right hand I have holden, to subdue nations before him, and I will loose the loins of kings,...
>
> I will go before thee, and make the crooked places straight: I will break in pieces the gates of brass, and cut in sunder the bars of iron:
>
> And I will give thee the treasures of darkness, and hidden riches of secret places....
>
> Isaiah 45:1-3

The statements that follow are some of my favorite Scriptures concerning the anointing. We subdue nations through the anointing. We loose the loins of kings. We are able to strip the power and authority of principalities and powers. We break in pieces the gates of brass, and cut in sunder the bars of iron. Walled cities with strong gates are opened unto us. We receive the treasures of darkness and hidden riches of secret places. The NEB says, *"I will give you treasures from dark vaults, hoarded in secret places."* There is much wealth hidden in the earth. We have access to this wealth through the anointing.

> The Spirit of the Lord GOD is upon me; because the LORD hath anointed me to preach good tidings unto the meek; he has sent me to heal the brokenhearted, to proclaim liberty to captives, and the opening of the prison to them that are bound.

> To proclaim the acceptable year of the LORD, and the day of vengeance of our God; to comfort all that mourn;
>
> Isaiah 61:1,2

> How God anointed Jesus of Nazareth with the Holy Ghost and with power: who went about doing good, and healing all that were oppressed of the devil; for God was with him.
>
> Acts 10:38

We are partakers of Christ's anointing. We are anointed to sit on the throne of David. We heal the sick and cast out devils. We also do good because of the anointing. We release vengeance upon the powers of darkness. We loose the prisoners. We heal the brokenhearted. We are anointed to preach the gospel. Allow these Scriptures on the anointing to saturate your spirit. Rise up in the anointing of the Holy Ghost and see miracles and breakthroughs. Understand and walk in revelation of the anointing.

Knowing We Have Been Established Upon David's Throne

> And David perceived that the Lord had established him king over Israel, and that he had exalted his kingdom for his people Israel's sake.
>
> 2 Samuel 5:12

David came to a place of realization that he was established by God on the throne. He had to endure much on his way to the throne. He probably had doubts that he would ever arrive. He finally came to a place of KNOWING. We must also come to a place of KNOWING. We must know in our spirits that we sit on David's throne. David had been anointed to be king years before by Samuel. He can now reign with confidence and authority. There is no more doubt in his mind. We must operate in faith and confidence from David's throne.

To be *established* means to be set. David no longer had to struggle and fight to possess his throne. He no longer had to run from Saul. His days of wandering came to an end. The same is true concerning you. God is settling us upon the throne. We are taking our place with authority and dominion. David's throne is established from generation to generation. Jesus now sits on this throne. He cannot be moved.

See yourself set strongly in your ministry or business. Allow no one to move you from your place. *You have been set by God.* This needs to be established firmly in your heart. Do not allow yourself to be double-minded. **Begin to rule and reign on the throne of David. Your enemies can no longer hold you back. Your day of delay is over. It is now time to enter into the fullness of your inheritance.**

Once you have been established, you can rule strongly. Others will recognize you. Your enemies will have to submit. There is no longer any doubt as to who is king. God will validate your ministry and anointing. Your position is established by God and recognized by men.

...upon this rock I will build my church; and the gates of hell shall not prevail against it.
Matthew 16:18

The Church has been established by God. The gates of hell cannot prevail against it. Your ministry is being established. Your church is being established. Your business is being established. The gates of hell cannot prevail against you.

Now there was long war between the house of Saul and the house of David: but David waxed stronger and stronger, and the house of Saul waxed weaker and weaker.
2 Samuel 3:1

There was long war between Saul and David before David was established on the throne. Maybe you have been in a long war. You must see yourself getting stronger while the enemy is getting weaker. This is a key to reigning, being established. God established David as king in spite of Saul. You are being established in spite of opposition.

Chapter 5
Prosperity on David's Throne
Resources are Released

Now I have prepared with all my might for the house of my God the gold for the things to be made of gold, and the silver for the things of silver, and the brass for the things of brass, the iron for the things of iron, and wood for the things of wood; onyx stones, and stones to be set, glistering stones, and of divers colors, and all manner of precious stones, and marble stones in abundance.

Moreover, because I have set my affection to the house of my God, I have of mine own proper good, of gold and silver, which I have given to the house of my God, over and above all that I have prepared for the holy house,

Even three thousand talents of gold, of the gold of Ophir, and seven thousand talents of refined silver, to overlay the walls of the houses withal.

1 Chronicles 29:2-4

We must set our affection to the house of God while sitting on David's throne. Great prosperity is released upon David's throne. There will be an abundance of resources released when we sit upon David's throne.

Both riches and honor come of thee, and thou reignest over all; and in thine hand is power and might; and in thine hand is to make great, and to give strength to all.

Now therefore, our God, we thank thee, and praise thy glorious name.

But who am I, and what is my people, that we should be able to offer so willingly after this sort? For all things come of thee, and of thine own have we given thee.

1 Chronicles 29:12-14

Remember David said these words while he was still on the throne. He knew that his prosperity came from the Lord. God's favor and mercy was upon his life. He walked in a covenant of prosperity. He willingly offered back to the Lord what came as a result of his blessing.

And he took their king's crown from off his head, the weight whereof was a talent of gold with precious stones: and it was set on David's head. And he brought forth the spoil of the city in great abundance.

2 Samuel 12:30

Solomon Prospers on David's Throne

Then sat Solomon upon the throne of David his father; and his kingdom was established greatly.

1 Kings 2:12

Wisdom and knowledge is granted unto thee; and I will give thee riches, and wealth, and honor,...

2 Chronicles 1:12

NOW the weight of gold that came to Solomon in one year was six hundred threescore and six talents of gold,

MOREOVER the king made a great throne of ivory, and overlaid it with the best gold.

AND all king Solomon's drinking vessels were of gold, and all the vessels of the house of the forest of Lebanon were of pure gold; none were of silver: it was nothing accounted of in the days of Solomon.

So king Solomon exceeded all the kings of the earth for riches and for wisdom.

And the king made silver to be in Jerusalem as stones, and cedars made he to be as the sycomore trees that are in the vale, for abundance.

1 Kings 10:14,18,21,23,27

Provision on David's Throne

And Hiram sent to Solomon, saying, I have considered the things which thou sentest to me for: and I will do all thy desire concerning timber of cedar, and concerning timber of fir.

My servants shall bring them down from Lebanon unto the sea: and I will convey them by sea in floats unto the place that thou shalt appoint me, and will cause them to be discharged there, and thou shalt receive them: and thou shalt accomplish my desire, in giving food for my household.

So Hiram gave Solomon cedar trees and fir trees according to all his desire.

1 Kings 5:8-10

But my God shall supply all your need according to his riches in glory by Christ Jesus.

Philippians 4:19

Whatever you lack God will provide through someone else. There is provision for you as you sit on the throne of David. Everything you need to fulfill your calling and commission is available to you as you sit on David's throne. God will give you favor with the individuals you need. Hiram gave Solomon all he needed to finish the temple. See yourself receiving all you need to do what God has commissioned you to do. There is provision on the throne of David.

There is much revelation concerning David's throne found in the prayers of David for Solomon. These prayers are found in Psalm 72. Jesus is the ultimate fulfillment of these prayers. We reign with Christ and also benefit from these prayers. David was praying prophetically for the Church.

Wealth Transfers on David's Throne

A good man leaveth an inheritance to his children's children: and the wealth of the sinner is laid up for the just.
Proverbs 13:22

For God giveth to a man that is good in his sight wisdom, and knowledge, and joy: but to the sinner he giveth travail, to gather and to heap up, that he may give to him that is good before God. This is also vanity and vexation of spirit.
Ecclesiastes 2:26

Though he heap up silver as the dust, and prepare raiment as the clay;

He may prepare it, but the just shall put it on, and the innocent shall divide the silver.
Job 27:16,17

The silver is mine, and the gold is mine, saith the LORD of hosts.
Haggai 2:8

...but money answereth all things.
Ecclesiastes 10:19

There is no lack on David's throne. Whatever we lack, God will transfer into our hands. Get ready for the wealth transfer. There *must* be a wealth transfer to fulfill these Scriptures. We are a part of the generation that will see ancient prophecies fulfilled.

Prepare yourself for the wealth transfer as you reign with Jesus from David's throne. The wealth of the wicked is laid up for the just. God gives to the sinner the job of heaping up for the righteous. There is a great amount of wealth being heaped up for the last days. There was much wealth transferred to David as a result of his victories. The gold and the silver belong to God.

Haggai speaks on the behalf of the LORD of hosts. God is a God of armies. His army on earth includes the Church. His heavenly army includes the angels. As the Church goes forth with angelic assistance, the gold and silver is being transferred. Begin to see wealth coming into your hands. Don't limit this to what you can see. There is a miraculous element to this transfer. Begin to confess these scriptures daily. This transfer is necessary for us to fulfill our commissions.

The Prophetic Prayers of David

David was a prophet and he prayed prophetically concerning his throne. These prayers are being answered today. We are the fulfillment of David's prayers through Jesus Christ.

> **Give the king thy judgments, O God, and thy righteousness unto the king's son.**
>
> **He shall judge thy people with righteousness, and thy poor with judgment.**
>
> **The mountains shall bring peace to the people, and the little hills, by righteousness.**
> *(A Psalm for Solomon)* **Psalm 72:1-3**

We are kings and priests unto God *(Revelation 5:10)*. We receive God's judgments by accessing the throne of David. We judge correctly because of the anointing we have received from Jesus, the Greater David. We are able to release righteous judgment into the earth. We issue apostolic and prophetic decrees. We execute righteousness in the earth. This is the authority the Church must walk in by accessing the throne of David.

We are called and anointed to bless the poor. We plead their case in intercession and defend them from the tyranny of evil. We preach the gospel to the poor.

He shall judge the poor of the people, he shall save the children of the needy, and shall break in pieces the oppressor.

They shall fear thee as long as the sun and moon endure, throughout all generations

Psalm 72:4,5

The Moffat translation says, *"May he prove the champion of the weak, may he deliver the forlorn, and crush the oppressor."* There is an anointing upon the throne of David to crush the oppressor. There is an anointing for deliverance of the poor and needy. This anointing is to continue from generation to generation. We break in pieces the oppressor and release the poor and needy from his grip as we rule and reign upon the throne of David.

He shall come down like rain upon the mown grass: as showers that water the earth.

In his days shall the righteous flourish; and abundance of peace so long as the moon endureth.

He shall have dominion also from sea to sea, and from the river to the ends of the earth

They that dwell in the wilderness shall bow before him; and his enemies shall lick the dust.

Psalm 72:6-9

Although David is praying for his son Solomon, these are prophetic prayers concerning the reign of Jesus through His Church. Jesus is the Seed of David. Solomon's reign is prophetic of the reign of Christ. He comes down like rain upon the grass and showers that water the grass. This is a revival anointing. We experience refreshing and revival as we sit upon the throne of David. The Moffat translation says, *"May his rule be like rainfall on the meadow."* The result will be the righteous flourishing. There is fruitfulness and abundance as we rule upon the throne of David.

There is also a dominion anointing as we sit upon the throne of David. This dominion extends to the ends of the earth. The enemies to David's throne lick the dust. David's foes bow before him. This is the prayer of David for his seed. We are the seed of David in Christ. This is the authority and dominion of the last-day Church. See yourself ruling and reigning with Christ upon the throne of David. See yourself flourishing. See yourself with an abundance of peace.

The kings of Tarshish and of the shall bring presents: the kings of Sheba and Seba shall offer gifts.

Yea, all the kings shall fall down before him: all nations serve him.
Psalm 72:10,11

Kings are under tribute to David's throne. Tribute is money paid regularly by one nation to another as acknowledgement of subjugation. It is something given to show gratitude, respect, honor, or praise. There is much wealth coming to David's throne in the form of tribute. Dominion brings tribute.

All nations come under this dominion. The end-time Church is called and anointed to subdue the nations. Our rule and reign covers the entire earth.

> For he shall deliver the needy when he crieth; the poor also, and him that hath no helper.
>
> He shall save the poor and needy, and shall save the souls of the needy.
>
> He shall redeem their soul from deceit and violence: and precious shall be their blood in their sight.
>
> Psalm 72:12-14

The DeWitt translation says, *"He will pity the wretched and needy."* We must have mercy and compassion as we sit on the throne of David. We deliver people with this compassion. We must rule with love and sympathy for the poor and needy. We are called to rescue those who have no one to help them. We cannot overlook the poor and needy as we sit upon the throne of David.

> And he shall live, and to him shall be given of the gold of Sheba: prayer shall be made for him continually; and daily shall he be praised.
>
> There shall be an handful of corn in the earth upon the top of the mountains; the fruit thereof shall shake like Lebanon: and they of the city shall flourish like grass of the earth.
>
> Psalm 72:15,16

There is a continuous reference to wealth coming to David's throne. The gold of Sheba comes. We know that the queen of Sheba brought gold to Solomon when she came to ask him hard questions (1 Kings 10). Other translations say the *"gold of Arabia."* We know today that much wealth is in the hands of Arabia. It will eventually come to the throne of David.

There is continuous prayer and intercession as we sit upon the throne of David. Prayer is a vital part of David's throne. We are to pray without ceasing. There is also continuous praise in David's house. The result is abundance. There is an abundance of corn and grain when we rule from David's throne. This is prosperity. We flourish like the trees of Lebanon.

> His name shall endure for ever: his name shall be continued as long as the sun: and men shall be blessed in him: all nations shall call him blessed.
>
> Blessed be the LORD God, the God of Israel, who only doeth wondrous things.
>
> And blessed be his glorious name for ever: and let the whole earth be filled with his glory; Amen and Amen.
>
> The prayers of David the son of Jesse are ended.
>
> Psalm 72:17-20

The name of the LORD is magnified as we rule and reign from the throne of David. All nations are blessed. This is a wonder to the earth. The whole earth is filled with His glory. This is the end of the prayers of David.

David is praying for the glory of God to be released throughout the earth. This is happening through His Church. The name of Jesus is being magnified through salvations, healings, and deliverances.

These prayers of David are prophetic prayers for the end-time Church. We are seeing the fulfillment of these prayers today. We are taking our place upon the throne of David and ruling and reigning with Jesus Christ.

Jehoshaphat Prospers on David's Throne

> NOW Jehoshaphat had riches and honor in abundance, and joined affinity with Ahab.
>
> 2 Chronicles 18:1

Don't join with the wrong people when you sit on David's throne. When this kind of prosperity comes into your life many will seek to join you. We need discernment as we sit on David's throne.

Uzziah Prospers on David's Throne

> ...and as long as he sought the LORD, God made him to prosper.
> 2 Chronicles 26:5

As long as Uzziah sought the Lord, he prospered. We must seek the Lord as we sit on David's throne. Everything we need will be added to us. Uzziah tapped into the prosperity vein that is on David's throne.

Hezekiah Prospers on David's Throne

> AND Hezekiah had exceeding much riches and honour: and he made himself treasuries for silver, and for gold, and for precious stones, and for spices, and for shields, and for all manner of pleasant jewels;
>
> Storehouses also for the increase of corn, and wine, and oil; and stalls for all manner of beasts, and cotes for flocks.
>
> Moreover he provided him cities, and possessions of flocks and herds in abundance: for God had given him substance very much.
> 2 Chronicles 32:27-29

Hezekiah was one of the godliest kings to sit on the throne of David. Every godly king that sat on this throne prospered. The ungodly kings did not prosper. Godliness is profitable. God delights in the prosperity of His servant. He will teach us to profit. We prosper even as our souls prosper. This is the will of God for His servants. See yourself prospering as you sit on the throne of David.

Chapter 6
Wisdom and Revelation on David's Throne

Wisdom is the principle thing...(Proverbs 4:7).
If any man lack wisdom let him ask of God...(James 1:5).

You cannot rule without wisdom A lack of wisdom will cause you to fail. Wisdom is the principle thing. This means it is the fundamental, basic, and primary thing. We have all the wisdom we need in Christ. He is our wisdom. In Him are hidden all the treasures of wisdom and knowledge. There is no lack of wisdom with God.

There is wisdom and revelation on David's throne. David received the pattern to build the house of God by revelation. He provided the pattern to his son Solomon.

> **THEN David gave to Solomon his son the pattern of the porch, and of the houses thereof, and of the treasuries thereof, and of the upper chambers thereof, and of the inner parlours thereof, and of the place of the mercy seat,**
>
> **And the pattern of all that he had by the spirit, of the courts of the house of the LORD, and all the chambers round about, of the treasuries of the house of God, and the treasuries of the dedicated things:**
>
> **All this, said David, the LORD made me understand in writing by his hand upon me, even all the works of this PATTERN.** 1 Chronicles 28:11,12,19

This pattern was revealed to David by the Spirit. We have access to the mysteries of the Kingdom when we sit upon David's throne. The hidden things are revealed. We need this revelation to build the house of the Lord properly. We need access to God's patterns and blueprints. We are called to be wise masterbuilders *(1 Corinthians 3:10)*.

And Solomon told her all her questions: there was not anything hid from the king, which he told her not.
1 Kings 10:3

Solomon had access to wisdom and revelation. There was nothing hid from him. Solomon was the wisest king to ever sit upon the throne of David, other than Jesus. His wisdom excelled all the wisdom of the wise men of his day. We should excel in wisdom. See yourself operating in wisdom and revelation as you sit upon the throne of David.

By me kings reign, and princes decree justice.
By me princes rule, and nobles, even all the judges of the earth.
Proverbs 8:15,16

We need God's wisdom to rule and reign on the throne of David. *The fear of the Lord is the beginning of wisdom* (Proverbs 9:10). We need the fear of the Lord to reign on David's throne. Wisdom is the principle thing. We have access to all the wisdom and revelation we need through Jesus Christ.

And he sought God in the days of Zechariah, who had understanding in the visions of God: and as long as he sought the LORD, God made him to prosper.
2 Chronicles 26:5

Uzziah had access to revelation as he sat upon the throne of David. We must seek God for wisdom as we sit upon the throne of David. Zechariah had understanding in the visions of God during Uzziah's reign.

This was a key to Uzziah's prosperity. Uzziah had divine insight through Zechariah. Zechariah instructed him in the things of God (Amplified Version).

Divine Guidance on David's Throne

THEN they told David, saying, Behold, the Philistines fight against Keilah, and they rob the threshingfloors.

Therefore David enquired of the LORD, saying, Shall I go up and smite these Philistines? And the LORD said unto David, Go, and smite the Philistines, and save Keilah.

Then David enquired of the LORD yet again. And the LORD answered him and said, Arise, go down to Keilah; for I will deliver the Philistines into thine hand.

So David and his men went to Keilah, and fought with the Philistines, and brought away their cattle, and smote them with a great slaughter. So David saved the inhabitants of Keilah.

1 Samuel 23:1,2,4,5

David received divine guidance concerning his battles and wars against his enemies. We have access to divine guidance as we sit upon the throne of David. A whole city was delivered by David. We can see cities delivered as we seek and obey the Word of the Lord. We see great miracles and breakthroughs through divine guidance. We receive our instructions from heaven and march accordingly.

The enemy is no match for us when we hear and follow the Word of the Lord. We need divine strategies as we sit on the throne of David. See yourself hearing God's voice on a consistent basis. Have confidence that God will hear your prayers and give you supernatural guidance.

> And let us bring again the ark of our God to us: for we inquired not at it in the days of Saul.
>
> 1 Chronicles 13:3

> So Saul died for his transgression which he committed against the LORD, even against the word of the LORD, which he kept not, and also for asking counsel of one that had a familiar spirit, to enquire of it:
>
> And enquired not of the LORD: therefore he slew him, and turned the kingdom unto David the son of Jesse.
>
> 1 Chronicles 10:13,14

> For as many as are led by the Spirit of God, they are the sons of God.
>
> Romans 8:14

David knew the importance of inquiring of the Lord. This was one of the greatest differences between him and Saul. Saul inquired of a witch and eventually lost his life. We must be led by the Spirit of God as we sit on David's throne. This was one of the keys to David's great success as a king. He was led by God in his decisions. He knew he needed supernatural direction. He depended upon God to give him directions.

> And the Philistines came and spread themselves in the valley of Rephaim.
>
> And David enquired of God, saying, Shall I go up against the Philistines? and wilt thou deliver them into mine hand? And the LORD said unto him, Go up; for I will deliver them into thine hand.
>
> So they came to Baal-perazim; and David smote them there. Then David said, God has broken in upon mine enemies by mine hand like the breaking forth of waters: therefore they called the name of that place Baal-perazim.
>
> 1 Chronicles 14:9-11

David received one of his greatest breakthroughs as a result of divine guidance. *Baal-perazim* means the Place of Breaking Through. The Taylor translation says, *"God used me to sweep away my enemies like water bursting through a dam."* We will also see great breakthroughs as we follow the leading of the Lord. We will sweep over our enemies like the breaking of a dam.

And the Philistines yet again spread themselves in the valley.

Therefore David enquired again of God; and God said unto him, Go not up after them; turn not away from them, and come upon them over against the mulberry trees.

And it shall be, when thou shalt hear a sound of going in the tops of the mulberry trees, that then shalt thou go out to battle: for God is gone forth before thee to smite the host of the Philistines.

David therefore did as God commanded him: and they smote the host of the Philistines from Gibeon even to Gazar.
1 Chronicles 14:13-16

This time God gave David a different strategy. We cannot become accustomed to doing things the same way all the time. God's strategies change. God may give you a different direction. Don't get stuck in routine. Be open to hear the voice of the Lord.

Trust in the LORD with all thine heart; and lean not unto thine own understanding.

In all thy ways acknowledge him, and he shall direct thy paths.
Proverbs 3:5,6

These have always been two of my favorite verses of scripture. They were the first verses I memorized as a believer. They are foundational verses to having success. We cannot lean to our own understanding. We must trust in the Lord for supernatural guidance as we sit on the throne of David.

AFTER all this, when Josiah had prepared the temple, Necho king of Egypt came up to fight against Charchemish by Euphrates: and Josiah went out against him.

But he sent ambassadors to him, saying, What have I to do with thee, thou king of Judah? I come not against thee this day, but against the house wherewith I have war: for God commanded me to make haste: forbear thee from meddling with God, who is with me, that he destroy thee not.

Nevertheless Josiah would not turn his face from him, but disguised himself, that he might fight with him, and hearkened not unto the words of Necho from the mouth of God, and came to fight in the valley of Megiddo.

And the archers shot at king Josiah; and the king said to his servants, Have me away; for I am sore wounded.

His servants therefore took him out of that chariot, and put him in the second chariot that he had; and they brought him to Jerusalem, and he died, and was buried in one of the sepulchres of his fathers. And all Judah and Jerusalem mourned for Josiah.

2 Chronicles 35:20-24

Sometimes the word of God comes through unsuspecting vessels. We must be sensitive to hear the voice of God no matter how it comes. Josiah lost his life because he did not recognize the voice of God through Necho, king of Egypt. One of Israel's greatest kings fell unnecessarily in battle. He did not have to die this way. We must be directed by God before making major decisions. Don't rush into things. Learn to seek and hear the voice of God while sitting on the throne of David.

Dreams and Visions on David's Throne

IN Gibeon the LORD appeared to Solomon in a dream by night: and God said, Ask what I shall give thee.

And Solomon awoke and behold it was a dream...
1 Kings 3:5,15

...your old men shall dream dreams, your young men shall see visions:
Joel 2:28

Dreams and visions are a part of David's throne. The Lord appeared to Solomon in a dream when he came to David's throne. He received the impartation of wisdom through a dream. Dreams are powerful. Solomon was a different man when he awoke from the dream.

We should expect dreams and visions as we sit upon the throne of David. There is access to this realm through David's throne. We can receive direction through dreams. We can be warned through dreams. We can receive revelation through dreams. We can receive impartation through dreams.

And he sought God in the days of Zechariah, who had understanding in the visions of God:...
2 Chronicles 26:5

Uzziah prospered through visions. Zechariah was the interpreter of visions during his reign. God speaks through his leaders through dreams and visions. This is a supernatural means of communication. God deals with kings in dreams and visions. He gave Pharaoh a dream. He spoke to Nebuchadnezzar in a dream. Joseph and Daniel were the interpreters of these dreams. We need the correct interpretations of the dreams and visions we receive. God will give us understanding in this realm.

NOW the rest of the acts of Hezekiah, and his goodness, behold, they are written in the vision of Isaiah the prophet,...
                              2 Chronicles 32:32

Isaiah was the visionary during the reign of Hezekiah. He had the vision of the Lord after the death of Uzziah. He was commissioned and sent through a vision. Visions reveal and release the purposes of God. We need to be visionaries as we sit on the throne of David. Visionaries are those who see visions. You are a visionary if you sit on the throne of David. Begin to see yourself as a visionary. You see into the future. You have insight into the plans and purposes of God.

Where there is no vision, the people perish:...
                              Proverbs 29:18

We need visions. Other translations say, *"the people cast off restraint."* People run wild without vision. Visions provide restraint for our lives. They cause us to be focused and disciplined. They release purpose and destiny. Be open to visions as you sit on the throne of David.

It is not expedient for me doubtless to glory. I will come to visions and revelations of the Lord.
                              2 Corinthians 12:1

This is the day of the restoration of apostolic and prophetic ministry. David was a prophet. He is also a type of apostolic ministry. The kings were types of apostles. With the restoration of the apostolic ministry, we are seeing a restoration of the understanding of dreams and visions. There is nothing hid from us as we sit upon the throne of David.

Chapter 7
Great Favor on David's Throne

I will pour upon the house of David...the spirit of grace favor and supplications.
        Zechariah 12:10

There is great favor upon David's throne. There is favor with God and man.

By this I know that thou favorest me, because my enemy doth not triumph over me.
        Psalm 41:11

This is a psalm of David. David knew God's favor. Favor protected him from his enemies.

LORD, by thy favor thou hast made my mountain to stand strong...
        Psalm 30:7

This is also a psalm of David. The Revised Standard Version says, *"By thy favor, O LORD, thou hast established me as a strong mountain."* David knew it was the favor of God that established him. God's favor establishes us as a strong mountain. This is a symbol of strength. Favor is grace. We have an abundance of grace as we sit on David's throne ...*in his favor is life:...* (Psalms 30:5).

We enjoy life when we sit on David's throne.

And Jesus increased in wisdom and stature, and in favour with God and man.
        Luke 2:52

Favor is a key to success. Favor is special and preferential treatment. We can have favor with God and man. We can increase in favor. God has favored you. Begin to confess favor. Walk in favor. I have written a small book entitled, *How to Tap into the Favor of God*.

Favor opens doors. Favor releases finances. Favor is the root for the word *favorite*. All of us have favorite foods and colors. We prefer and like these things. See yourself as one of God's favorites. David was one of God's favorite kings. You tap into this favor through Jesus Christ as you sit on the throne of David.

Praising God, and having favour with all the people. And the Lord added to the church daily such as should be saved.

Acts 2:47

The early Church had favor. This caused explosive church growth. Favor can cause your ministry to expand and grow. It can cause your business to expand and grow. We can tap into this favor as we sit on the throne of David.

Let not mercy and truth forsake thee: bind them about thy neck; write them on the table of thine heart:

So shalt thou find favour and good understanding in the sight of God and man.

Proverbs 3:3,4

Favor is increased in your life as you operate in mercy and truth. You will have favor from God and man. We must operate in mercy and truth as we sit upon the throne of David. Mercy is compassion. The Word of God is truth. Truth is also integrity and good faith. These attributes will release an abundance of favor in your life.

Esther received favor from the king. This brought deliverance to the Jews. Favor is powerful. It can change the course of nations. God will give you favor as you take your place on the throne of David.

Fame on David's Throne

And the fame of David went out into all lands; and the LORD brought the fear of him upon all nations.
1 Chronicles 14:17

...Saul has slain his thousands, and David his ten thousands.
1 Samuel 18:7

David was a famous king. His exploits brought him fame. He was famous in Israel for killing Goliath. Everyone knew who David was. His name spread to all the nations.

Fame comes with David's throne. Jesus had fame (*Luke 4:14*). Fame is not necessarily a bad thing. Don't be afraid of fame. God will make us famous. Fame means a reputation, especially for good. To be *famous* means to be eminent, foremost, honored, reputable, exalted, leading, noteworthy, outstanding, distinguished, and excellent. This is a part of David's throne.

There are many references to the fame of Jesus. His miracles brought him fame. It was noised abroad that he was in the city. Wherever he went people followed him. They followed him into the desert when he tried to withdraw. He had compassion on them and healed their sick.

When people came to hear Jesus they had an expectation because of his fame. Many came believing and received miracles because of his fame. Fame creates an atmosphere for miracles. Fame creates an expectation in the hearts of the people.

Fame gives you influence. We are called to influence our generation. Fame attracts. It attracts people and wealth. Multitudes were attracted to Jesus because of his fame. They came from distant places to hear his preaching and teaching. They followed him into the wilderness.

> And Solomon's wisdom excelled the wisdom of all the children of the east country, and all the wisdom of Egypt.
> ...and his fame was in all the nations round about.
> 1 Kings 4:30,31

Solomon was famous for his wisdom. This is a good thing. Wisdom releases fame. Solomon sat on David's throne. The Queen of Sheba came because of his fame. Many will be drawn to us because of the fame that comes with David's throne.

> AND when the queen of Sheba heard of the fame of Solomon concerning the name of the LORD, she came to prove him with hard questions.
>
> And she came to Jerusalem with a very great train, with camels and bare spices, and very much gold, and precious stones:...
>
> And when the queen of Sheba had seen all Solomon's wisdom, and the house that he had built,
>
> And the meat of his table, and the sitting of his servants, and the attendance of his ministers, and their apparel, and his cupbearers, and his ascent by which he went up into the house of the LORD; there was no more spirit in her.
>
> And she said to the king, It was a true report that I heard in mine own land of thy acts and of thy wisdom.
>
> Howbeit I believed not the words, until I came, and mine eyes had seen it: and, behold, the half was not told: thy wisdom and thy prosperity exceedeth the FAME which I heard.
> 1 Kings 10:1,2,4-7

> And Jehoshaphat waxed GREAT exceedingly;...
> 2 Chronicles 17:12

And the Ammonites gave gifts to Uzziah: and his name spread abroad even to the entering in of Egypt; for he strenghthened himself exceedingly.

2 Chronicles 26:8

Both Jehoshaphat and Uzziah waxed great upon David's throne. Greatness is a part of David's throne. God will give us a name. Synonyms for great include majestic, dignified, famous, celebrated, distinguished, renowned, prominent, and preeminent.

...thy gentleness has made me great.

Psalm 18:35

David knew about greatness. The New American Bible says, *"and you have stooped to make me great."* The Moffat version says, *"thine answers to prayer have raised me."*

And David went on, and grew great, and the LORD God of hosts was with him.

2 Samuel 5:10

Chapter 8
A Praying and Prophectic Generation

Answered Prayer on David's Throne

I will pour out upon the house of David, the spirit of grace and SUPPLICATIONS.

…prayer also shall be made for him continually;…

…and let the whole earth be filled with his glory; Amen, and Amen.

The prayers of David, the son of Jesse, are ended.

Psalm 72:15,19,20

Pray without ceasing.   1 Thessalonians 5:17

The house of David is a house of prayer. David was a man of prayer. He was a seeker of God. *This is the spirit of David.* God's house is a house of prayer for all nations.

…But Hezekiah prayed for them, saying, The good LORD pardon every one

That prepareth his heart to seek God, the LORD God of his fathers, though he be not cleansed according to the purification of the sanctuary.

And the LORD hearkened to Hezekiah, and healed the people.   2 Chronicles 30:18-20

> **Whose soever sins ye remit, they are remitted unto them; and whose soever sins ye retain, they are retained.**
>
> **John 20:23**

Hezekiah prayed for the people and God healed them. You have great authority in prayer as you sit on the throne of David. You have the power to remit or retain sins. Your prayers release healing. Your prayers release forgiveness. You operate as a king and priest upon the throne of David.

David prayed for his throne. He prayed for his son Solomon. This is recorded in Psalm 72. His prayer was that the earth would be filled with his glory. He cried unto God for deliverance. The Psalms are filled with the prophetic prayers of David.

We must pray while on David's throne. There is a spirit of supplication upon David's throne. This is the spirit of prayer. We are praying for the earth to be filled with God's glory. We are praying for the nations. We are seeing a revival of worldwide prayer and intercession.

Jesus, the Greater David, rebuked them for turning the house of prayer into a den of thieves. They had turned God's house into a house of merchandise. Jesus was known for his prayer life. He prayed until there fell from him great drops of blood. Jesus offered up prayers and supplications with strong crying and tears *(Hebrews 5:7)*.

> **AND when Jesus departed thence, two blind men followed him, crying, and saying, Thou Son of David, have mercy on us.**
>
> **Matthew 9:27**

Two blind men made supplication to Jesus, the son of David. Notice that mercy is connected to David. Jesus, the Greater David, healed them. He responded to their supplication in mercy. Supplications release the mercy of God. This can include salvation, healing, protection, and rescue.

> **The LORD hath heard my supplication; the LORD will receive my prayer.**
>
> **Let all mine enemies be ashamed and sore vexed: let them return and be ashamed suddenly.**
>
> **Psalm 6:9,10**

David's supplication brought him deliverance from his enemies. God's mercy was released through supplications. We can ask for the Lord's mercy through our supplication. David knew the power of prayer and supplication as he sat on the throne.

Solomon Prays Upon the Throne of David

> **Yet have thou respect unto the prayer of thy servant, and to his supplication, O LORD my God, to hearken unto the cry and to the prayer, which thy servant prayeth before thee to day:**
>
> **1 Kings 8:28**

This is the prayer of Solomon concerning the house of the Lord. God appeared to Solomon the second time and confirmed His promise to the house of David. God responded to the prayers and supplications of David and Solomon. He will also respond to our prayers as we sit upon the throne of David.

> **And the LORD said unto him, I have heard thy prayer and thy supplication, that thou hast made before me: I have hallowed this house, which thou hast built, to put my name there for ever; and mine eyes and mine heart shall be there perpetually.**
>
> **1 Kings 9:3**

Even the wicked king Manasseh was heard by the Lord when he humbled himself and prayed on David's throne.

> And when he was in affliction, he besought the LORD his God, and humbled himself greatly before the God of his fathers,
>
> And prayed unto him: and he was intreated of him, and heard his supplication, and brought him again to Jerusalem into his kingdom. Then Manasseh knew that the LORD he was God.
>
> 2 Chronicles 33:12,13

Manasseh experienced the sure mercies of David. He was one of Israel's most wicked kings. God had him removed to Babylon. In his affliction he sought the Lord. His prayer and supplication was heard by God. Our prayers and supplications will also be heard by God as we tap into the sure mercies of David.

The Holy Spirit is a Spirit of prayer. He is a Spirit of intercession. He has been sent to help us pray. He knows what is the mind of the spirit. He helps us pray according to the will of God.

We Have Access to the Prophetic on David's Throne

> AND the LORD spake unto Gad, David's seer, saying,
>
> 1 Chronicles 21:9

> And he set Levites in the house of the LORD with cymbals, with psalteries, and with harps, according to the commandment of David, and of Gad the kings' seer, and Nathan the prophet: for so was the commandment of the LORD by his prophets.
>
> 2 Chronicles 29:25

Gad was David's seer. Nathan was a prophet that ministered to David. This was one of the keys to David's greatness. David had access to the prophetic while he sat upon the throne. These prophetic leaders helped David establish worship in the tabernacle. The prophetic ministry was a major part of David's tabernacle *(1 Chronicles 25).*

The name *Gad* means a *troop.* It is a prophetic picture of a company of prophets that are connected to David's throne. God is raising up an army of prophets that minister in David's house. David's house is the Church. David received and was blessed by the ministry of Gad.

GAD, a troop shall overcome him: but he shall overcome at the last.
Genesis 49:19

This is Jacob's prophecy over Gad. It is a play on words of his name which means a troop. He is saying a troop shall overcome a troop. Gad would be overcome, but he would overcome at the end. Gad will overcome in the last days. The last-day Church shall see Gad restored with an overcoming ability. After years of neglect, we are seeing a restoration of the prophetic ministry. God is raising up an army of prophetic people that will minister on David's throne.

AND of Gad he said, Blessed be he that enlargeth Gad: he dwelleth as a lion, and teareth the arm with the crown of the head.

And he provided the first part for himself, because there, in a portion of the lawgiver, was he seated; and he came with the heads of the people, he executed the justice of the LORD, and his judgments with Israel.
Deuteronomy 33:20,21

God is enlarging Gad. The prophetic movement is expanding. Prophetic teams are being raised up around the globe. Prophets are also being raised up as never before. The New American Standard Bible translation says, *"Blessed be he that has made Gad so vast."* The Jerusalem translation says, *"Blessed be he that who gives*

Gad space." God is giving Gad space. There is room for Gad in the house of David. We must have Gad if we are going to sit on the throne of David.

Gad is like a lion. This represents ferocity, boldness, and courage. He tears off arm and scalp *(Deuteronomy 33:20).* This is what Gad does to his enemy. The arm and the crown of the head represents authority. A lion is also a symbol of the apostolic ministry.

Gad receives a commander's portion. This is the portion of the lawgiver. Gad has authority. The prophets' ministry needs to be in the leadership of the Church. Gad is an honored leader. We need to make room for the prophetic in the leadership of the Church if we are to rule on David's throne.

Gad came with the heads of the people. This is another reference to leadership. The Berkeley translation says, *"he went with the chiefs of the nation."* God executes the justice and judgment of the LORD.

> **And when Asa heard these words, and the prophecy of Oded the prophet, he took courage, and put away the abominable idols out of all the land of Judah and Benjamin, and out of the cities which he had taken from Mount Ephraim, and renewed the altar of the LORD, that was before the porch of the LORD.**
>
> **2 Chronicles 15:8**

Asa took courage after hearing the words of Oded the prophet. He had access to the prophetic anointing as he sat upon the throne of David. Asa later ended up in trouble because of rejection of the prophetic.

> **Then Asa was wroth with the seer, and put him in a prison house; for he was in a rage with him because of this thing,...**
>
> **2 Chronicles 16:10**

A Praying and Prophectic Generation

We must receive and take heed to the prophetic while on David's throne. The prophetic ministry will cause us to hear God's voice and walk accordingly. Those who sit on David's throne need the encouragement and direction that comes from the prophetic ministry.

But Jehoshaphat said, Is there not here a prophet of the LORD besides, that we might enquire of him?

2 Chronicles 18:6

THEN upon Jahaziel the son of Zechariah, the son of Benaiah, the son of Jeiel, the son of Mattaniah, a Levite of the sons of Asaph, came the Spirit of the LORD in the midst of the congregation.

2 Chronicles 20:14

Jehoshaphat also drew from the prophetic anointing as he sat on the throne of David. This prophetic word released deliverance from his enemies. The kings who did not listen to the prophets ended up in trouble.

Chapter 9
Returning the Ark of God

The Presence of God on David's Throne

And the ark of God remained with the family of Obed-edom in his house three months. And the LORD blessed the house of Obed-edom, and all that he had.
1 Chronicles 13:14

SO David, and the elders of Israel, and the captains over thousands, went to bring up the ark of the covenant of the LORD out of the house of Obed-edom with JOY.
1 Chronicles 15:25

David brought the ark of God from Obed-edom's house to Jerusalem when he ascended to the throne. Obed-edom's house had been blessed by the presence of the Ark. David desired this blessing and determined to bring the Ark to Zion. He placed the ark under a tent, which was David's tabernacle. The Ark represents the presence of God. We need the presence of God as we sit on David's throne. We are the generation that returns the ark of God.

After this will I return, and will build again the tabernacle of David, which is fallen down; and I will build again the ruins thereof, and I will set it up:

> That the residue of men might seek after the Lord, and all the Gentiles, upon whom my name is called, saith the Lord, who doeth all these things.
>
> **Acts 15:16,17**

God is rebuilding the tabernacle of David. The tabernacle of David is a type of the New Testament Church. The result will be all the Gentiles seeking God.

The Ark was hidden behind a curtain in Moses' tabernacle. Only the high priest had access to it once a year. Not so in David's Tabernacle. All the priests and Levites had access to the presence of God in David's tabernacle. David was an Old Testament man that tapped into New Testament worship.

> Arise, O LORD, into thy rest; thou, and the ark of thy strength.
>
> Let thy priests be clothed with righteousness; and let thy saints shout for joy.
>
> For thy servant David's sake turn not away the face of thy anointed.
>
> **Psalm 132:8-10**

The Ark represents the strength of God. The priests were the guardians of the Ark. We must guard and carry the ark of God while sitting on the throne of David. There was great rejoicing when David brought the Ark to Jerusalem. David danced before the Lord with all his might. There is joy and rejoicing in the house of David. We are anointed with the oil of gladness as we sit upon the throne of David.

We must rule on David's throne with gladness. The joy of the Lord is our strength (Nehemiah 8:10). Sadness and depression has no place on David's throne. There is joy, gladness, celebration, praise and worship in David's tabernacle. This is Davidic praise and worship. We have seen a restoration of Davidic worship in the church. There is a spirit of liberty being released upon us to praise! We are praising God with all our might! We are free to praise in David's house!

> **Thus all Israel brought up the ark of the covenant of the LORD with shouting,...**
> **1 Chronicles 15:28**

The ark was brought up with shouting. Davidic churches have a shout. God goes up with a shout (Psalms 47:5). Great power is released through shouting. Walls come down through shouting. Don't underestimate the power of the shout. Shouting belongs to kings. The king's arrival would be proceeded by a shout.

> ...shout unto God with the voice of triumph.
> **Psalm 47:1**

> ...and let thy saints shout for joy.
> **Psalm 132:9**

> ...her saints shout aloud for joy.
> **Psalm 132:16**

There is prophetic worship in David's tabernacle. New songs are birthed by the Holy Spirit.

> **MOREOVER David and the captains of the host separated to the service of the sons of Asaph, and of Heman, and of Jeduthun, who should PROPHESY with harps, with psalteries, and with cymbals: and the number of the workmen according to their service was:**
>
> **Of the sons of Asaph; Zaccur, and Joseph, and Nethaniah, and Asarelah, the sons of Asaph under the hands of Asaph, which PROPHESIED according to the order of the king.**
>
> **Of Jeduthun: the sons of Jeduthun; Gedaliah, and Zeri, and Jeshaiah, Hashabiah, and Mattithiah, six, under the hands of their father Jeduthun, who PROPHESIED with a harp, to give thanks and to praise the LORD.**
> **1 Chronicles 25:1-3**

There was prophetic music and singing in David's tabernacle. David was a psalmist. He prophesied in song. Davidic worship is prophetic. Our music and songs need a prophetic dimension. We can prophesy and decree the will of God in song. We need anointed minstrels and psalmists. They help us to rule and reign on David's throne.

Speaking to yourselves in psalms and hymns and spiritual songs, singing and making melody in your heart to the Lord.

Ephesians 5:19

Sing unto him a new song; play skillfully with a loud noise.

Psalm 33:3

O SING unto the LORD a new song...

Psalm 96:1

And he spake three thousand proverbs: and his songs were a thousand and five.

1 Kings 4:32

This is New Testament worship. We are to sing new songs. These are songs birthed by the Holy Spirit. These are spiritual songs. They do not originate from the flesh or soul, but from the spirit. David wrote many songs. So did his son Solomon.

Chapter 10
A Generation That Recovers All

Restoration on David's Throne

David recovered all....

1 Samuel 30:19

And he shall send Jesus Christ, which before was preached unto you:

Whom the heaven must receive until the times of restitution of all things, which God hath spoken by the mouth of all his holy prophets since the world began.

Acts 3:20,21

The prophets have foretold of these days. We are living in days of restoration. We are recovering all. We must restore and recover what the enemy has taken as we sit on the throne of David. To *restore* means to recover, mend or repair. It means to build up again that which has been torn down.

And they that shall be of thee shall build the old waste places: thou shalt raise up the foundations of many generations; and thou shalt be called, The repairer of the breach, The restorer of paths to dwell in.

Isaiah 58:12

The Taylor translation says, *"You will be known as 'The People Who Rebuild Their Walls and Cities."*

We are people of restoration. The godly kings in the line of David moved in restoration. To restore also means to bring back to health or strength. We are repairers of the breach and restorers of paths to dwell in.

> AND all the people of Judah took Azariah, which was sixteen years old, and made him king instead of his father Amaziah.
>
> He built Elath, and RESTORED it to Judah, after that the king slept with his fathers.
>
> 2 Kings 14:21,22

We are called to restore what the enemy has taken. Restoration is a part of the apostolic ministry. We are living in a day of the restoration of the five-fold ministry, including apostles and prophets. God is restoring the years that the locust, cankerworm, palmerworm, and caterpillar have eaten (Joel 2:25). Restoration always follows desolation.

> And to masons, and hewers of stone, and to buy timber and hewed stone to REPAIR THE BREACHES of the house of the LORD, and for all that was laid out for the house to repair it.
>
> 2 Kings 12:12

> And the king and Jehoiada gave it to such as did the work of the service of the house of the LORD, and hired masons and carpenters to REPAIR the house of the LORD, and also such as wrought iron and brass to MEND the house of the LORD.
>
> 2 Chronicles 24:12

This occurred during the reign of Joash. We are seeing the restoration of the house of the Lord. All the ministries and gifts that belong in God's house are being restored. We must move in restoration truth as we sit upon the throne of David.

> And Ahaz gathered together the vessels of the house of God, and cut in pieces the vessels of the house of God, and shut up the doors of the house of the LORD, and he made him altars in every corner of Jerusalem.
> 2 Chronicles 28:24

> **HE in the first year of his reign, in the first month, opened the doors of the house of the LORD, and REPAIRED them.**
> 2 Chronicles 29:3

This occurred during the reign of Hezekiah. The house of God had fallen into decay during the reign of his father Ahaz. Hezekiah moved in restoration when he sat upon the throne of David.

> **And the children of Israel that were present at Jerusalem kept the feast of unleavened bread seven days with great gladness:...**
> 2 Chronicles 30:21

Hezekiah restored the feast of passover and unleavened bread. The people celebrated the feast with gladness. Restoration is always a time of great gladness. We are seeing a restoration of the feasts of the LORD. These feasts were prophetic pictures of life in Christ. We have the real thing. Feasts are times of great joy and celebration. They are times of gathering. They are times of receiving the blessing of the LORD.

> **And let them deliver it into the hand of the doers of the work, that have the oversight of the house of the LORD:...**
>
> **Unto carpenters, and builders, and masons, and to buy timber and hewn stone to repair the house.**
> 2 Kings 22:5,6

This was the commandment of King Josiah. He desired to restore the house of the Lord. This was after the desolations brought on by the reigns of Manasseh and Amon before him. We must repair the damage done by previous generations. Jesus brings restoration. We must flow with him in the spirit of restoration. This is the Nehemiah anointing. Daniel prayed for restoration. We must also pray for restoration.

Executing Judgment on David's Throne

O house of David, thus saith the LORD; Execute judgment in the morning, and deliver him that is spoiled out of the hand of the oppressor, lest my fury go out like fire, and burn that none can quench it, because of the evil of your doings.
Jeremiah 21:12

God loves judgment. Judgment brings deliverance to them that are oppressed. This is the responsibility of the house of David. We are called to execute judgment on the behalf of those who are oppressed.

For there are set thrones of judgment, the thrones of the house of David.
Psalm 122:5

Judgment is a part of David's throne. We are called to execute *judgments* against wickedness as we sit upon David's throne. We have the authority to do so. David executed judgment and justice through his kingdom. Judgment involves issuing sentences and passing verdicts. The wicked hate judgment. The righteous love judgment.

A king that sitteth in the throne of judgment scattereth away all evil with his eyes.
Proverbs 20:8

The New American Standard Bible translation says, *"dispels all evil with his glance."* The Septuagint says, *"nothing that is evil can stand before his eyes."* The king searches out any evil in his kingdom with his eyes.

There is nothing hidden from his glance. Nothing is hidden from us when we sit upon David's throne. When we discern and cast out devils, we are executing judgment against the powers of darkness.

The eyes represent discernment. We have discernment when we sit upon David's throne. We scatter evil with our eyes. We are not ignorant of Satan's devices. We understand the operation of the enemy. See yourself operating in discernment as you sit upon the throne of David.

...his eyes were as a flame of fire;
Revelation 1:14.

This is a picture of Jesus as our judge. His eyes were as a flame of fire. The Taylor translation says, *"His eyes penetrated as a flame of fire."* There is an anointing to see through the wicked as we sit on David's throne. We sit with Jesus as kings that scatter away evil with our eyes.

And Asa did that which was right in the eyes of the LORD, as did David his father.

And he took away the sodomites out of the land, and removed all the idols that his father had made.

And also Maachah his mother, even her he removed from being queen, because she had made an idol in a grove; and Asa destoyed her idol, and burnt it by the brook Kidron.

1 Kings 15:11-13

This is judgment. Asa executed judgment against the Sodomites and idols of the land. He even removed his own mother from her position as queen. We must use our authority against wicked spirits as we sit upon David's throne. Executing judgment is a function of the king. We are to have no mercy upon the powers of darkness.

Josiah Executes Judgment on David's Throne

> And they brake down the altars of Baalim in his presence, and the images, that were on high above them, he cut down; and the groves, and the carved images, and the molten images, he brake in pieces, and must dust of them, and strowed it upon the graves of them that had sacrificed unto them.
>
> And he burnt the bones of the priests upon their altars, and cleansed Judah and Jerusalem.
>
> 2 Chronicles 34:4,5

Josiah executed judgment against idolatry and false religion when he ascended to David's throne. He burned the bones of the false priests. Fire represents judgment. He purged Judah and Jerusalem. He beat down and broke in pieces. He utterly destroyed the images and idols of the land.

> And he put down the idolatrous priests, whom the kings of Judah had ordained to burn incense in the high places in the cities of Judah, and in the places round about Jerusalem; them also that burned incense unto Baal, to the sun, and to the moon, and to the planets, and to all the host of heaven.
>
> 2 Kings 23:5

He removed the idolatrous priests from their positions.

> And he brought out the grove from the house of the LORD, without Jerusalem, unto the brook Kidron, and burned it at the brook Kidron, and stamped it small to powder, and cast the powder thereof upon the graves of the children of the people.
>
> And he brake down the houses of the sodomites, that were by the house of the LORD, where the women wove hangings for the grove.
>
> 2 Kings 23:6,7

Josiah executed judgment against the idolatry and perversion in the land. He burnt the grove and stamped it to powder. This is complete destruction. He executed judgment with zeal. He had no mercy upon the idolatry of the land. Idolatry is demonic. This should be our attitude toward everything demonic, especially that which is close to the house of the Lord. We have authority to execute this judgment as we sit upon the throne of David.

And he brought all the priests out of the cities of Judah, and defiled the high places where the priests had burned incense, from Geba to Beersheba, and brake down the high places of the gates that were in the entering in of the gate of Joshua the governor of the city, which were on a man's left hand at the gate of the city.

Nevertheless the priests of the high places came not up to the altar of the LORD in Jerusalem, but they did eat of the unleavened bread among their brethren.

2 Kings 23:8,9

Josiah next dealt with the priests. He judged those that had burned incense in the high places. He destroyed the high places. God anoints us to destroy the high places as we reign with Jesus on the throne of David. We have the authority to remove that which is not ordained of God.

And he defiled Tophet, which is in the valley of the children of Hinnom, that no man might make his son or his daughter to pass through the fire to Molech.

And he took away the horses that the kings of Judah had given to the sun, at the entering in of the house of the LORD, by the chamber of Nathan-melech the chamberlain, which was in the suburbs, and burned the chariots of the sun with fire.

2 Kings 23:10,11

Josiah executed judgment against the worship of the sun and against Molech. These were abominations. We are called to execute judgment against the abominations of the land. Josiah is operating in the spirit of judgment and burning (Isaiah 4:4). This spirit needs to be released from the throne of David.

> **And the altars that were on the top of the upper chamber of Ahaz, which the kings of Judah had made, and the altars which Manasseh had made in the two courts of the house of the LORD, did the king beat down, and brake them down from thence, and cast the dust of them into the brook Kidron.**
>
> **2 Kings 23:12**

Josiah executes judgment against that which had been established in previous generations. Sometimes we have to deal with things that were erected in the past. This is especially true of false religion. These things were connected to the house of the LORD. Ahaz and Manasseh allowed idolatry and witchcraft to flourish in the land. God raised up Josiah to sit on David's throne and execute judgment against the wickedness of previous generations.

> **And the high places that were before Jerusalem, which were on the right hand of the mount of corruption, which Solomon the king of Israel had builded for Ashtoreth the abomination of the Zidonians, and for Chemosh the abomination of the Moabites, and for Milcom the abomination of the children of Ammon, did the king defile.**
>
> **And he brake in pieces the images, and cut down the groves, and filled their places with the bones of men.**
>
> **2 Kings 23:13,14**

Josiah deals with what had been established by Solomon after he departed from the Lord. These were strongholds that had been in the land for generations. The kings of Israel had opened the door for this by not exercising their authority in a godly way. It takes a man of authority to undo what was established by authority. Josiah was using his authority upon the throne of David to execute vengeance upon the idols of the land.

MOREOVER the altar that was at Bethel, and the high place which Jeroboam the son of Nebat, who made Israel to sin, had made, both that altar and the high place he brake down, and burned the high place, and stamped it small to powder, and burned the grove.

2 Kings 23:15

Josiah executed judgment against the false altar of Jeroboam. This altar had become a snare to Israel. It was established by the authority of a king and was destroyed by the authority of a king. We have kingly authority through Jesus Christ. We must also execute judgment against false altars. Altars represent worship.

Josiah also burned the grove. This was the idol of Asherah. It was a sacred pole that was worshipped by Israel. This would be the equivalent of a present day obelisk. These represent strongholds of lust and perversion.

And Josiah turned himself, he spied the sepulchres that were there in the mount, and sent, and took the bones out of the sepulchres, and burned them upon the altar, and polluted it, according to the word of the LORD which the man of God proclaimed, who proclaimed these words.

Then he said, What title is that I see? And the men of the city told him, It is the sepulchre of the man of

God, which came from Judah, and proclaimed these things that thou hast done against the altar of Bethel.

And he said, Let him alone; let no man move his bones. So they let his bones alone, with the bones of the prophet that came out of Samaria.

2 Kings 23:16,18

Josiah did not consider what was unholy as sacred. He burned the bones of the false priests upon the altar of Beth-el. He executed judgment against a religious spirit. He respected the bones of the prophet who prophesied hundreds of years before concerning the judgment of God against the idolatry of Jeroboam. We must execute judgment against wickedness as we rule and reign on the throne of David.

And all the houses also of the high places that were in the cities of Samaria, which the kings of Israel had made to provoke the LORD to anger, Josiah took away, and did to them according to all the acts that he had done in Bethel.

And he slew all the priests of the high places that were upon the altars, and burned men's bones upon them, and returned to Jerusalem.

2 Kings 23:19,20

The Amplified version says, *"to defile the places forever."* To defile means to profane. These high places could no longer be used. He executed judgment against them completely. We rule with Jesus upon the throne and execute judgments against the high places.

MOREOVER the workers with familiar spirits, and the wizards, and the images, and the idols, and all the abominations that were spied in the land of Judah and in Jerusalem, did Josiah put away, that he might perform the words of the law which were written in the book that Hilkiah the priest found in the house of the LORD.

And like unto him was there no king before him. that turned to the LORD with all his heart, and with all his soul, and with all his might, according to the law of Moses; neither after him arose any like him.

2 Kings 23:24,25

Josiah executed judgment against witchcraft. This was according to the Word of the LORD. He removed from the land wizards and those with familiar spirits. This was forbidden by the law of Moses. He had the authority to do so as the king of Israel. He did it with a complete heart. We need a perfect heart as we sit on the throne of David. We also have authority to execute judgments against the spirits of witchcraft.

We have the authority to root out, pull down, throw down, and destroy.

Chapter 11
A Generation That Wars Like David

Warfare on David's Throne

Blessed be the LORD my strength, which teacheth my hands to war, and my fingers to fight:

My goodness, and my fortress; my high tower, and my deliverer; my shield, and he in whom I trust; who subdueth my people under me.

Psalm 144:1,2

There is warfare on David's throne. God taught David's hands to war and his fingers to fight. God subdued the people under him. We must see ourselves upon the throne of David. God will also teach our hands to war and our fingers to fight. David was a man of war. There was much warfare during David's reign. David's natural enemies are types of our spiritual enemies. God will also give us victory over our enemies as we sit with Jesus on the throne of David.

I have pursued mine enemies, and overtaken them: neither did I turn till they were consumed.

I have wounded them that they were not able to rise: they are fallen under my feet.

For thou hast girded me with strength unto the battle: thou hast subdued under me those that rose up against me.

Thou hast also given me the necks of mine enemies; that I might destroy them that hate me.
                                              Psalm 18:37-40

This is the spirit of David. David was a mighty warrior. He pursued and destroyed his enemies. His strength came from God. He was anointed for warfare. God subdued his enemies under him. We can also have the necks of our enemies. We defeat our enemies through our leader Jesus Christ. The DeWitt translation says, *"And those that hate me I utterly destroy."*

David consumed his enemies. He did not turn until they were completely destroyed. We must see our spiritual enemies completely destroyed. We must pursue the enemy. To *pursue* means to follow in order to overtake or capture. It means to chase with hostile intent. We must be aggressive on David's throne. *We cannot be passive when it comes to warfare.*

David was a man of dominion. He subdued nations. Strangers submitted to his authority.

Great deliverance giveth he to his king; and sheweth mercy to his anointed, to David and to his seed for evermore.
                                                 Psalm 18:50

This is one of my favorite verses in relation to David. Great deliverance means great victories, great triumphs, and glorious conquests. This deliverance is given to David and to his seed. *We are the seed of David through Jesus Christ.* We can also receive this great deliverance as we sit upon the throne of David.

For at that time day by day there came to David to help him, until it was a great host, like the host of God.

All these men of war, that could keep rank, came with a perfect heart to Hebron, to make David king

over Israel: and all the rest also of Israel were of one heart to make David king.
1 Chronicles 12:22,38

God will send you help as you sit on the throne of David. David had a host like the host of God. It was a formidable force. It was like the army of God. David was established as king by warring men. He had an army of fighting men supporting him in his kingdom.

AND when the Philistines heard that David was anointed king over Israel, all the Philistines went up to seek David. And David heard of it, and went out against them.

And the Philistines came and spread themselves in the valley of Rephaim.
1 Chronicles 14:8,9

The enemy may challenge your authority. David did not draw back but went out to meet the enemy. One of the responsibilities of kings is to lead the people into battle. We need not fear the enemy when we sit upon David's throne. Jesus is our champion. He is the true David. He leads us into battle against our enemies.

Second Samuel chapter eight gives examples of David's exploits over his enemies.

AND after this it came to pass that David smote the Philistines, and subdued them: and David took Metheg-ammah out of the hand of the Philistines.
2 Samuel 8:1

The Moffat translation says, *"he took the supreme power from the Philistines."* Methegammah was the mother city of the Philistines. It was a metropolis. A metropolis is a main city or capital. It is any large or important city. David took a main city out of the hands of the Philistines.

> And he smote Moab, and measured them with a line, casting them down to the ground; even with two lines measured he to put to death, and with one full line to keep alive. And so the Moabites became David's servants, and brought gifts.
> **2 Samuel 8:2**

David measured out their fate by lot. He determined their fate and operated in complete authority over the Moabites.

> David smote also Hadadezer, the son of Rehob, king of Zobah, as he went to recover his border at the river Euphrates.
>
> David took from him a thousand chariots, and seven hundred horsemen, and twenty thousand footmen: and David houghed all the chariot horses, but reserved of them for an hundred chariots.
> **2 Samuel 8:3,4**

Chariots are a symbol of strength. It would be the equivalent of a modern day tank. David took the chariots from Hadadezer and destroyed them saving one hundred for himself. He completely immobilized the enemy.

> And when the Syrians of Damascus came to succour Hadadezer king of Zobah, David slew of the Syrians two and twenty thousand men.
>
> And David put garrisons in Syria of Damascus: and the Syrians became servants to David, and brought gifts. And the Lord preserved David whithersoever he went.
>
> And David took the shields of gold that were on the servants of Hadadezer, and brought them to Jerusalem.
>
> And from Betah, and from Berothai, cities of Hadadezer, king David took exceeding much brass.
> **2 Samuel 8:5-8**

David destroyed Hadadezer's reinforcements. The Moffat translation says, *"wherever David went, the Eternal gave him victory."* We can have victory after victory while we sit on David's throne. No matter how many enemies come against us, we can have victory through Jesus Christ.

WHEN Toi king of Hamath heard that David had smitten all the host of Hadadezer,

Then Toi sent Joram his son unto king David, to salute him, and to bless him, because he had fought against Hadadezer, and smitten him: for Hadadezer had wars with Toi. And Joram brought with him vessels of silver, and vessels of gold, and vessels of brass:

Which also king David did dedicate unto the LORD, with the silver and gold that he had dedicated of all nations which he subdued;

Of Syria, and of Moab, and of the children of Ammon, and of the Philistines, and of Amalek, and of the spoil of Hadadezer, son of Rehob, king of Zobah.
2 Samuel 8:9-12

David enjoyed the spoils of victory. He dedicated these spoils unto the LORD. We too can enjoy the spoils of victory as we sit on David's throne. There are great blessings that come from warfare. Each victory releases spoils for the kingdom of God.

And David gat him a name when he returned from smiting of the Syrians in the valley of salt, being eighteen thousand men.

AND he put garrisons in Edom; throughout all Edom put he garrisons, and all they of Edom became David's servants. And the LORD preserved David withersoever he went.
2 Samuel 8:13,14

David was known for his victories. David won a name for himself through his victories. His victory over the Syrians in the valley of salt established his name. There are certain victories that cause our name to be recognized.

So David waxed greater and greater: for the LORD of hosts was with him.
1 Chronicles 11:9

In that day shall the LORD defend the inhabitants of Jerusalem; and he that is feeble among them at that day shall be as David; and the house of David shall be as God, as the angel of the LORD before them.
Zechariah 12:8

Even the feeble will be as David in our day. The Davidic anointing is resting upon the Church. The house of David will be as God. What a tremendous word to the Church! The weak will be strong! The spirit of might is being released in our day.

Strongholds Fall to David's Throne

AND the king and his men went to Jerusalem unto the Jebusites, the inhabitants of the land: which spake unto David, saying, Except thou take away the blind and the lame, thou shalt not come in hither: thinking, David cannot come in hither.

Nevertheless, David took the strong hold of Zion: the same is the city of David.
2 Samuel 5:6,7

The enemy will attempt to mock you as you sit on David's throne. The Jebusites mocked David. They felt their city was secure. But David took the stronghold of Zion. There are strongholds that you will take as you sit on the throne of David. See yourself pulling down strongholds. A stronghold is a fortress. It is a fortified place. These places will fall before Jesus in you. Don't be intimidated by the enemy. He will fall before the anointing on your life. We have been anointed to pull down strongholds.

David's Mighty Men

THESE also the chief of the mighty men whom David had, who strengthened themselves with him in his kingdom, and with all Israel, to make him king, according to the word of the LORD concerning Israel.

And this is the number of the mighty men whom David had: Jashobeam, an Hachmonite, a chief of the captains: he lifted up his spear against three hundred slain by him at one time.

1 Chronicles 11:10,11

Joshabeam lifted up his spear against three hundred at one time. He was one of David's mighty men. A spirit of might is released upon David's throne. David's mighty men were also known for exploits. The same spirit that was upon David rested upon them.

And after him was Eleazar the son of Dodo, the Ahohite, who was of the three mighties.

He was with David at Pas-dammim, and there the Philistines were gathered together to battle, where was a parcel of ground full of barley; and the people fled from before the Philistines.

And they set themselves in the midst of that parcel, and delivered it, and slew the Philistines; and the LORD saved them by a great deliverance.

1 Chronicles 11:12-14

David's mighty men helped David against his enemies. You are not alone on David's throne. There are other believers who help us to fight while we are on the throne. We must set ourselves against the enemy. God will also give us great deliverance.

NOW three of the thirty captains went down to the rock to David, into the cave of Adullam; and the host of the Philistines encamped in the valley of Rephaim.

And David was then in the hold, and the Philistines' garrison was then at Bethlehem.

And David longed, and said, Oh that one would give me drink of the water of the well of Bethlehem, that is at the gate!

And the three brake through the host of the Philistines, and drew water out of the well of Bethlehem, that was by the gate, and took it, and brought it to David: but David would not drink of it, but poured it out to the LORD,

And said, My God forbid it me, that I should do this thing: shall I drink the blood of these men that have put their lives in jeopardy? for with the jeopardy of their lives they brought it. Therefore he would not drink it. These things did these three mightiest.
1 Chronicles 11:15-19

David's mighty men were loyal to him. Three of his captains risked their lives to get him a drink of water from the well of Bethlehem. They broke through the host of the Philistines to get to the well. David would not drink the water, but poured it out as an offering to the Lord. These three mighty men distinguished themselves in this feat. They were fearless and committed to their leader. We must be fearless and committed to Jesus Christ.

AND Abishai the brother of Joab, he was chief of the three: for lifting up his spear against three hundred, he slew them, and had a name among the three.

Of the three, he was more honourable than the two; for he was their captain: howbeit he attained not to the first three.
1 Chronicles 11:20,21

Abishai was more famous than the thirty, but he attained not to the fame of the first three. He lifted up his spear against three hundred men and killed them. David's men did exploits. We are called to do exploits as we sit on David's throne. Abishai won a name for his feat. We should also win a name for our feats. We are a part of David's mighty men through Jesus Christ.

> Benaiah the son of Jehoiada, the son of a valiant man of Kabzeel, who had done many acts; he slew two lionlike men of Moab: also he went down and slew a lion in a pit in a snowy day.
>
> And he slew an Egyptian, a man of great stature, five cubits high; and in the Egyptian's hand was a spear like a weaver's beam; and he went down to him with a staff, and plucked the spear out of the Egyptian's hand, and slew him with his own spear.
>
> These things did Benaiah the son of Jehoiada, and had the name among the three mighties.
>
> Behold, he was honorable among the thirty, but attained not to the first three: but David set him over his guard.
>
> 1 Chronicles 11:22-25

David's mighty men are prophetic pictures of end-time believers. We are called to do the greater works of Christ. See yourself as a mighty man or woman of God. The same spirit that was upon David rested upon these men. The spirit of Christ rests upon us. Benaiah slew two lionlike men and a lion. He also slew an Egyptian with his own spear. These are types of Satan and demons. The Egyptian was over seven feet tall. We are called to slay giants.

First Chronicles chapters 11 and 12 lists the mighty men of David. They are identified. God is identifying his mighty men today. You are on the list. Your name is written in the Lamb's book of life. Begin to see yourself as an end-time warrior reigning with Christ on David's throne.

All these men of war, that could keep rank, came with perfect heart to Hebron, to make David king over Israel: and all the rest also of Israel were of one heart to make David king.

1 Chronicles 12:38

Uzziah Wars on David's Throne

And he went forth and warred against the Philistines and break down the wall of Gath, and the wall of Jabneh, and the wall of Ashdod, and built cities about Ashdod, and among the Philistines.

Moreover Uzziah had an host of fighting men, that went out to war by bands, according to the number of their account by the hand of Jeiel the scribe and Maaseiah the ruler,...

The whole number of the chief of the fathers of the mighty men of valour were two thousand and six hundred.

And under their hand was an army, three hundred thousand and seven thousand and five hundred, that made war with mighty power, to help the king against the enemy.

And Uzziah prepared for them throughout all the host shields, and spears, and helmets, and habergeons, and bows, and slings to cast stones.

And he made in Jerusalem engines, invented by cunning men, to be on the towers and upon the bulwarks, to shoot arrows and great stones withal. And his name spread far abroad; for he was marvellously helped, till he was strong.

2 Chronicles 26:6,11-15

Uzziah was a strong general. He equipped his army and warred from David's throne. He led a host of fighting men. This is prophetic of the end-time Church. We are seeing an army of believers who will war according to the commandment of our King Jesus. Warfare is a part of the throne of David.

BUT when he was strong, his heart was lifted up to his destruction: for he transgressed against the LORD his God, and went into the temple of the LORD to burn incense upon the altar of incense.
2 Chronicles 26:16

We must be careful to remain humble on David's throne. Strength and power can lead to pride. The enemy could not defeat Uzziah, but pride was able to bring him down. We must give glory to the LORD for every victory. The Knox translation says, *"But this greatness of his made his heart proud to his own undoing."*

Jotham Wars on David's Throne

HE fought also with the king of the Ammonites, and prevailed against them. And the children of Ammon gave him the same year a hundred talents of silver, and ten thousand measures of wheat, and ten thousand of barley. So much did the children of Ammon pay unto him, both the second year, and the third.

So Jotham became mighty, because he prepared his ways before the LORD his God.
2 Chronicles 27:5,6

Jotham subdued the Ammonites and received tribute from them. You must see yourself subduing your enemies as you sit upon David's throne.

Chapter 12
A Kingdom Dominion Generation

Dominion on David's Throne

God hath spoken in his holiness; I will rejoice, I will divide Shechem, and mete out the valley of Succoth.

Gilead is mine, and Manasseh is mine; Ephraim also is the strength of mine head; Judah is my lawgiver;

Moab is my washpot; over Edom will I cast out my shoe: Philistia, triumph thou because of me.

Psalm 60:6-8

David was a man of dominion. He ruled and reigned over his enemies. Christ rules over his enemies. All dominions shall serve and obey him (Daniel 7:27). He is the greater David. We rule and reign with Christ on the throne of David.

I saw in the night visions, and, behold, one like the Son of man came with the clouds of heaven, and came to the Ancient of days, and they brought him near before him.

And there was given him DOMINION, and glory, and a kingdom, that all people, nations, and languages, should serve him: his dominion is an everlasting dominion, which shall not pass away, and his kingdom that shall not be destroyed.

Daniel 7:13,14

David's throne extends beyond Israel to the entire earth through Jesus Christ. All people, nations, and languages come under His dominion. We have an anointing and authority to touch and impact nations. This is a part of the dominion of the Church. We are called to go to the uttermost parts of the earth. Davidic, end-time churches shall impact nations.

> **Thou madest him to have dominion over the works of thy hands; thou hast put all things under his feet:**
> **Psalm 8:6**

> **Thou hast put all things in subjection under his feet. For in that he put all in subjection under him, he left nothing that is not under him. But we see not yet all things put under him.**
> **Hebrews 2:8.**

There is still much rebellion in the earth. We have not yet seen the full manifestation of these Scriptures. All things are subject unto us. We are marching toward the complete fulfillment. Jesus will return from heaven and reign as KING OF KINGS. We are reigning and will reign with Him on the throne of David. We are TRAINING FOR REIGNING. Learn to rule and reign *now*. Begin to have a dominion mentality!

> **AND I will cut off the chariot from Ephraim, and the horse from Jerusalem, and the battle bow shall be cut off: and he shall speak peace unto the heathen: and his dominion shall be from the sea even to sea, and from the river even to the ends of the earth.**
> **Zechariah 9:10**

The reign of Christ is a reign of peace. We are called to establish peace in the hearts of men. The kingdom of God is righteousness, peace, and joy in the Holy Ghost (Romans 14:17). This is being released to the ends of the earth. See yourself ruling and reigning with Christ on the throne of David, dispensing peace to the nations. See yourself breaking the powers of darkness. See yourself cutting off the chariot and battle bow of the enemy.

> **AND it came to pass when the king sat in his house, and the LORD had given him rest round about from all his enemies;**
> **2 Samuel 7:1**

Although there was much warfare on David's throne, the Lord eventually gave him rest. There is a season of rest that comes after you subdue your enemies. Rest is the result of dominion. See yourself entering into the rest that results from dominion. Many of the enemies that fought you in the past will no longer be able to vex you. God is putting our enemies under our feet. God subdued David's enemies and gave him peace. We will see the same thing as we sit on the throne of David.

> **And when the servants of Hadarezer saw that they were put to the worse before Israel, they made peace with David, and became his servants:...**
> **1 Chronicles 19:19**

Begin to see your enemies making peace with you. This is the result of dominion. Those that hated you will come and bow down before you. All enemies are subject to David's throne.

Taking the Crown of the Enemy

> **And David took the crown of their king from off his head, and found it to weigh a talent of gold, and there were precious stones in it; and it was set upon David's head: and he brought also exceedingly much spoil out of the city.**
> **1 Chronicles 20:2**

A crown represents authority and dominion. David took the crown from his enemy and set it on his own head. You can seize the crown of the enemy and place it on your head. This is dominion. See yourself seizing the enemies authority. We are dethroning principalities and powers through Jesus Christ. All the kingdoms around David became subject to him.

Solomon's Dominion

> **For he had dominion over all the region on this side the river, from Tisphsah even to Azzah, over all the kings on this side the river: and he had peace on all sides round about him.**
> **1 Kings 4:24**

> **But now the LORD my God hath given me rest on every side, so that there is neither adversary nor evil occurent.**
> **1 Kings 5:4**

Solomon inherited the throne of his father David and experienced dominion. Peace is a sign of dominion. Peace is the result of subduing the enemy. We have peace as we sit on the throne of David.

> **He hath delivered my soul in peace from the battle that was against me: for there were many with me.**
> **Psalm 55:18**

> **He maketh peace in thy borders, and filleth thee with the finest of the wheat.**
> **Psalm 147:14**

Our borders represent our dominion. God gives peace within our borders. We solidify and completely subdue the enemy in our territory. This is our sphere of authority. All believers and churches have a sphere of authority. Learn to rule in your sphere. Subdue the enemy in your territory.

We have a dominion mandate. Warfare is for the purpose of establishing peace. We cannot have peace as long as the enemy abounds. We war in order to subdue.

We are called to establish the kingdom of God in the hearts of men which is a kingdom of peace.

For the mountains shall depart, and the hills be removed; but my kindness shall not depart from thee, neither shall the covenant of my peace be removed, saith the LORD that hath mercy on thee.
Isaiah 54:10

We have a covenant of peace. This is the result of the kindness and mercy of the Lord. This covenant of peace cannot be removed. It is a firm covenant. Solomon enjoyed peace during his reign. He benefited from the sure mercies of David.

Chapter 13
Excellence and Order on David's Throne

And they ministered before the dwelling place of the tabernacle of the congregation with singing, until Solomon had built the house of the LORD in Jerusalem: and then they waited on their office according to their ORDER.
                                                   1 Chronicles 6:32

There was order in David's kingdom. Chaos and disorder are not of God. Our lives and ministries need to be in order. First Chronicles chapter 23 through 28 talks about David's kingdom and its order. David divided the courses of the priests and Levites and set them in order. There was also order in his army. David divided the priests into 24 course (1 Chronicles 25:31). This is a governmental number. It is a number that represents the apostolic ministry.

David gave this order to his son Solomon (1 Chronicles 28:13). David set up Israel's order for worship. This order was followed for generations to come. David learned the importance of order in bringing the ark of God to Zion.

> And David called for Zadok and Abiathar the priests, and for the Levites, for Uriel, Asaiah, and Joel, Shemiah, and Eliel, and Amminadab,

> And said unto them, Ye are the chief of the fathers of the Levites: sanctify yourselves, both ye and your brethren, that ye may bring up the ark of the LORD God of Israel unto the place that I have prepared for it.
>
> For because ye did it not at the first, the LORD our God made a breach upon us, for that we sought him not after the DUE ORDER.
>
> 1 Chronicles 15:11-13

There must be order on David's throne if we are to carry the ark of God. The Ark represents the presence of God. We are carriers of God's glory. Things must be set properly in our lives and ministries. Order causes things to run smoothly and efficiently.

> Of the increase of his government and peace there shall be no end, upon the throne of David, and upon his kingdom, TO ORDER IT, and to establish it with judgment and with justice from henceforth even for ever. The zeal of the LORD of hosts will perform this.
>
> Isaiah 9:7

We sit on the throne of David with Jesus. There is order in this kingdom. To *order* means to set up properly, to establish correctly. Dominion and prosperity come with this order. Order prepares us for increase. Unto him that has shall more be given. The opposite of order is confusion. God is not the author of confusion.

> Although my house be not so with God; yet he hath made with me an everlasting covenant, ORDERED IN ALL THINGS, and SURE...
>
> 2 Samuel 23:5

The An American Translation translation says, *"Set in order in all things and secured."* God has ordered David's house. His kingdom has been set and ordered by God. Order helps keep our position sure.

This is seen during the reign of Solomon.

> And when the queen of Sheba had seen all Solomon's wisdom, and the house that he had built,
>
> And the meat of his table, and the sitting of his servants, and the attendance of his ministers, and their apparel, and his cupbearers, and his ascent by which he went up into the house of the LORD; there was no more spirit in her.
>
> 1 Kings 10:4,5

We need order and excellence as we sit on David's throne. The queen of Sheba was so impressed until there was no more spirit in her. The Jerusalem translation says, *"the organisation of his staff and the way they were dressed."* The Knox translation says, *"the order and splendor of his court."* When the queen of Sheba saw the order and excellence in Solomon's court, there was no breath left in her.

Hezekiah set the service of the house of the LORD in order.

> …So the service of the house of the LORD was set in order.
>
> And Hezekiah rejoiced, and all the people, that God had prepared the people: for the thing was done suddenly.
>
> 2 Chronicles 29:35,36

Hezekiah had to restore the order of David to the kingdom. Years of idolatry, desolation, and neglect had destroyed this order. Apostolic ministries set things in order. They restore order to the house of God. This allows the full blessings of God to flow.

> For this cause left I thee in Crete, that thou shouldest SET IN ORDER the things that are wanting, and ordain elders in every city, as I had appointed thee.
>
> Titus 1:5
>
> …And the rest will I set in order when I come.
>
> 1 Corinthians 11:34

> ...let all things be done decently and in order.
> 1 Corinthians 14:40

Order is defined as the condition in which everything is in its place and working properly. Excellence is the fact or state of excelling or superiority.

Great Deliverance on David's Throne

> Great deliverance giveth he to his king; and sheweth mercy to his anointed, to David, and to his seed for evermore.
> Psalm 18:50

There is great salvation and deliverance on David's throne. Salvation is healing, deliverance, wholeness, and protection. The Psalms of David are filled with references to deliverance.

> For thou hast delivered my soul from death, mine eyes from tears, and my feet from falling.
> Psalm 116:8

> He delivered me from my strong enemy, and from them which hated me: for they were too strong for me.
> Psalm 18:17

David had many enemies. They were strong and hated his throne. David enjoyed deliverance from these enemies, and so can we. We have access to deliverance as we sit on David's throne. God delivered David from the hand of Saul. He delivered him from the hand of Absalom. He delivered him from the plots and conspiracies of his enemies. We have been delivered from the power of darkness (Colossians 1:13).

We have been sent to preach deliverance to the captives. Jesus ministered deliverance to thousands. He cast out devils and healed the sick. He sent his twelve disciples to do the same. We partake of Christ's anointing. We have been sent to bring deliverance to the captives. See yourself with a powerful deliverance ministry as you sit on David's throne. See yourself breaking the jaws of the wicked and setting the captives free. See yourself crushing the oppressor as David did. Jesus, the greater David, lives in you.

> **But upon mount Zion shall be deliverance....**
> **Obadiah 1:17**

We live on Mount Zion. God rules out of Zion. Zion was the residence of King David. There is deliverance on Mount Zion. Our churches must have deliverance. There is deliverance in David's house and on David's throne. Deliverance is escape. It is rescue. Multitudes will escape and be rescued as we rule and reign upon the throne of David. Nations will be delivered.

Deliverance is a result of God's mercy. Deliverance is the result of redemption. We have been redeemed from the hand of the enemy. We have been bought back with the blood of Jesus. We have been delivered from death and hell. We have been delivered from all of our fears. We have been delivered from destruction. This includes sickness and disease. This is a part of the sure mercies of David.

David understood the need for God's deliverance as he sat upon the throne. He knew he needed God's protection. He could not trust in horses and chariots like the heathen kings. He trusted in the Lord for his deliverance. We must also trust in the Lord's deliverance as we sit upon the throne of David.

> **Thou art my hiding place; thou shalt preserve me from trouble; thou shalt compass me about with songs of deliverance. Selah.**
> **Psalm 32:7**

David praised God for deliverance. We must also praise God for deliverance. Many of the songs of David spake of the Lord's deliverance. He was encompassed with songs of deliverance.

Beware of Pride While Sitting on the Throne of David

When pride cometh, then cometh shame:...
Proverbs 11:2

Pride goeth before destruction, and a haughty spirit before a fall.
Proverbs 16:18

Pride is one of the deadliest enemies to David's throne. Pride opens the door for the spirits of destruction and shame. Some of the greatest kings of Israel fell victim to pride. God will promote us and bless us as long as we walk in humility.

...I humbled my soul with fasting....
Psalm 35:13

David knew the power of humility. It was one of his greatest strengths as a king. He humbled his soul with fasting. Fasting is a biblical way to humble one's soul. Learn to fast while sitting on the throne of David.

Fasting is a powerful discipline that humbles the soul.

BUT when he was strong, his heart was lifted up to his destruction: for he transgressed against the LORD his God, and went into the temple of the LORD to burn incense upon the altar of incense.
2 Chronicles 26:16

God prospered Uzziah and gave him victory over his enemies. When he was strong he fell victim to the deadly spirit of pride. He transgressed and went into the temple to burn incense. This right was only reserved for the priests. He was smitten with leprosy and was a leper until the day of his death. God judged him for his pride.

> But Hezekiah rendered not again according to the benefit done unto him; for his heart was lifted up: therefore there was wrath upon him, and upon Judah and Jerusalem.
>
> 2 Chronicles 32:25

Hezekiah was one of Israel's greatest kings. Toward the end of his reign he too fell victim to the deadly spirit of pride. Judah and Jerusalem suffered as a result of his pride.

> And at that time Berodach-baladan, the son of Baladan, king of Babylon, sent letters and a present unto Hezekiah: for he had heard that Hezekiah had been sick.
>
> And Hezekiah hearkened unto them, and shewed them all the house of his precious things, the silver, and the gold, and the spices, and the precious ointment, and all the house of his armour, and all that was found in his treasures: there was nothing in his house, nor in all his dominion, that Hezekiah shewed them not.
>
> THEN came Isaiah the prophet unto king Hezekiah, and said unto him, What said these men? and from whence came they unto thee? And Hezekiah said, They are come from a far country, even from Babylon.
>
> 2 Kings 20:12-14

And he said, What have they seen in thine house? And Hezekiah answered, All the things that are in mine house have they seen: there is nothing among my treasures that I have not shewed them.

And Isaiah said unto Hezekiah, Hear the word of the LORD.

> Behold, the days come, that all that is in thine house, and that which thy fathers have laid up in store unto this day, shall be carried into Babylon: nothing shall be left, saith the LORD.
>
> 2 Kings 20:15-17

> HOWBEIT in the business of the ambassadors of the princes of Babylon, who sent unto him to enquire of the wonder that was done in the land, God left him, to try him, that he might know all that was in his heart.
>
> 2 Chronicles 32:31

Pride will cause you to make deadly mistakes while on the throne. Hezekiah revealed all his wealth to the ambassadors of Babylon. This revealed the pride in his heart. The Babylonians would eventually come and take this wealth away. God tried him through the ambassadors of Babylon. God will also test our hearts as we prosper on the throne of David. We must be able to handle the wealth and fame that comes through David's throne. Humility is necessary to rule and reign on the throne of David.

> A man's pride shall bring him low: but honour shall uphold the humble in spirit.
>
> Proverbs 29:23

God hates pride. It is an abomination unto him. He that exalts himself shall be abased. He that humbles himself shall be exalted. Pride has no place on the throne of David. God resists the proud (1 Peter 5:5). Arrogance, haughtiness, and boasting will hinder us from reigning. Humility is one of the greatest strengths of a ruler. Learn to rule by humility. Humility is not a weakness, but a strength.

> Now I Nebuchadnezzar praise and extol and honour the King of heaven, all whose works are truth, and his ways judgment: and those that walk in pride he is able to abase.
>
> Daniel 4:37

Humility brings honor. Prides brings one low. The New American Standard Bible translation says, *"Man's pride causes his humiliation, but he who is humble of spirit obtains honor."* To humiliate means to bring low, fill with shame, or degrade. Nebuchadnezzar was brought low because of his pride. He was driven from among men and acted like a beast. When he returned to his senses, he recognized and worshipped the God of Israel. This is the testimony of a king.

> **And it shall be, when he sitteth upon the throne of his kingdom, that he shall write him a copy of this law in a book out of that which is before the priests the Levites:**
>
> **And it shall be with him, and he shall read therein all the days of his life: that he may learn to fear the LORD his God, to keep all the words of this law and these statutes, to do them:**
>
> **That his heart be not lifted up above his brethren, and that he turn not aside from the commandment, to the right hand, or to the left: to the end that he may prolong his days in his kingdom, he, and his children, in the midst of Israel.**
>
> **Deuteronomy 17:18-20**

These are instructions for sitting upon the throne. We must keep the Word of God before our eyes. We must read the Word all the days of our lives. This will prevent our hearts from being lifted up. The king was not exempt from this. The Torah says, *"Thus he will not act haughtily towards his fellows."* The Word of God is our rule. It is our standard as we rule upon the throne of David. Read the Word. Meditate in the Word. It is the key to reigning.

Beware of the Flesh While Sitting on the Throne of David

This I say then, Walk in the Spirit, and ye shall not fulfill the lust of the flesh.
Galatians 5:16

Neither shall he multiply wives to himself, that his heart turn away....
Deuteronomy 17:17

And David perceived that the LORD had established him king over Israel, and that he had exalted his kingdom for his people Israel's sake.

AND David took him more concubines and wives out of Jerusalem, after he was come from Hebron....
2 Samuel 5:12-13

God warned the kings not to multiply wives to themselves. Power is dangerous. David began to multiply wives unto himself. He was not satisfied with what he had. He later took Uriah's wife and had him murdered. We cannot yield to the flesh while we sit on David's throne. Lust is another deadly enemy to David's throne.

Many kings would multiply wives for political purposes. They would enter into treaties with other nations and intermarry to form alliances. This is what happened to Solomon.

BUT king Solomon loved many strange women, together with the daughter of Pharaoh, women of the Moabites, Ammonites, Edomites, Zidonians, and Hittites;

And he had seven hundred wives, princesses, and three hundred concubines: and his wives turned away his heart.

For it came to pass, when Solomon was old, that his wives turned away his heart after other gods: and his

> heart was not perfect with the LORD his God, as was the heart of his father David.
>
> **1 Kings 11:1,3**

Solomon's wives turned his heart away from God. Solomon, the wisest king of Israel, began to follow idols. He built high places in Jerusalem. The kingdom was divided because of Solomon's sin. We cannot allow the flesh to turn away our heart from the Lord. We must walk in the Spirit if we are to rule and reign with Jesus on the throne of David.

> **And Rehoboam loved Maachah the daughter of Absalom above all his wives and his concubines: (for he took eighteen wives, and threescore concubines: and begat twenty and eight sons, and threescore daughters.)**
>
> **2 Chronicles 11:21**

Rehoboam, the son of Solomon, continued in the tradition of marrying many wives. He forsook the law of the Lord. There are generational spirits that we need to deal with. We cannot yield to the sins of the fathers. We must break the cycles and curses from our past in order to rule and reign on the throne of David.

Beware of Ungodly Soul Ties While Sitting on the Throne of David

> **NOW Jehoshaphat had riches and honour in abundance, and joined affinity with Ahab.**
>
> **2 Chronicles 18:1**

> **Be not unequally yoked together with unbelievers: for what fellowship hath righteousness with unrighteousness? And what communion hath light with darkness?**
>
> **2 Corinthians 6:14**

Relationships are important as we sit on the throne of David. We are the result of our relationships.

Jehoshaphat made the mistake of joining with Ahab. Jehoshaphat's son would marry Ahab's daughter. This was a political arrangement that was disastrous for Judah. Ungodly soul ties are deadly enemies to David's throne.

He that walketh with wise men shall be wise: but a companion of fools shall be destroyed.

Proverbs 13:20

Ungodly soul ties can lead to destruction. We must have right relationships as we sit on the throne of David. Solomon's relationships with strange women caused him to go astray. People have influence on us for good or evil. See yourself in the right relationships. Pray for godly relationships that bless your life, business, and ministry.

So Jonathan made a covenant with the house of David, saying, Let the LORD even require it at the hand of David's enemies.

And Jonathan caused David to swear again, because he loved him as he loved his own soul.

1 Samuel 20:16,17

David and Jonathan were covenant friends. Jonathan helped David escape from Saul. Jonathan loved David as his own soul. This is an example of a godly soul tie. Covenant relationships are necessary as we sit on the throne of David.

Forty and two years old was Ahaziah when he began to reign, and he reigned one year in Jerusalem. His mother's name was Athaliah the daughter of Omri.

He also walked in the ways of the house of Ahab: for his mother was his counsellor to do wickedly.

Wherefore he did evil in the sight of the LORD like the house of Ahab: for they were his counsellors after the death of his father to his destruction.

HE walked also after their counsel, and went with Jehoram the son of Ahab king of Israel to war against Hazael king of Syria at Ramoth-gilead: and the Syrians smote Joram.

And he returned to be healed in Jezreel because of the wounds which were given him at Ramah, when he fought with Hazael king of Syria. And Ahaziah the son of Jehoram king of Judah went down to see Jehoram the son of Ahab at Jezreel, because he was sick.

And the destruction of Ahaziah was of God by coming to Joram: for when he was come, he went out with Jehoram against Jehu the son of Nimshi, whom the LORD had anointed to cut off the house of Ahab.

And it came to pass, that, when Jehu was executing judgment upon the house of Ahab, and found the princes of Judah, and the sons of the brethren of Ahaziah, that ministered to Ahaziah, he slew them.

And he sought Ahaziah: and they caught him, (for he was hid in Samaria,) and brought him to Jehu: and when they had slain him, they buried him: Because, said they, he is the son of Jehoshaphat, who sought the LORD with all his heart. So the house of Ahaziah had no power to keep still the kingdom.
2 Chronicles 22:2-9

BLESSED is the man that walketh not in the counsel of ungodly,...
Psalm 1:1

We cannot walk in the counsel of the ungodly as we sit on David's throne. Ahaziah was counseled by his mother Athaliah to do wickedly. He joined forces with Jehoram the son of Ahab. He lost his life because of this relationship. He was killed by Jehu as he was executing judgment on the house of Ahab. We must be careful who we receive counsel from as we sit on the throne of David.

> **For by wise counsel thou shalt make war: and in the multitude of counselors there is safety.**
> **Proverbs 24:6**

> **And Ahithophel was the king's counselor: and Hushai the Archite was the king's companion:**
> **1 Chronicles 27:33**

> **Now the counsel of Ahithophel, which he counseled in those days, was as if a man had inquired at the oracle of God: so was all the counsel of Ahithophel both with David and with Absalom.**
> **2 Samuel 16:23**

Ahithophel was David's counselor. This was another key to David's success as a king. Ahithophel's counsel was as the Word of God. We need Ahithophel's counsel as we sit on the throne of David. Counselors release the wisdom of God. They help us to rule and reign upon the throne. God will give you wise counsel as you sit upon the throne of David.

> **And Joash did that which was right in the sight of the LORD all the days of Jehoiada the priest.**
> **2 Chronicles 24:2**

> **Now after the death of Jehoiada came the princes of Judah, and made obeisance to the king. Then the king hearkened unto them.**
>
> **And they left the house of the LORD God of their fathers, and served groves and idols: and wrath came upon Judah and Jerusalem for this their tresspass.**
> **2 Chronicles 24:17,18**

Joash had a godly mentor in Jehoiada the priest. He served God faithfully as long as Jehoiada was alive. He listened to the wrong counsel after Jehoiada's death. Their counsel caused him to forsake the Lord. He ended up being murdered in his kingdom. Wrong counsel can lead to destruction.

Jehoiada is a type of an apostolic ministry. He was a father to Joash. He gave him correct counsel. We need apostolic relationships that give us wise counsel. We must be aware of wrong relationships as we sit on the throne of David.

Beware of Satan as You Sit on the Throne of David

AND Satan stood up against Israel, and provoked David to number Israel.   **1 Chronicles 21:1**

And God was displeased with this thing; therefore he smote Israel.   **1 Chronicles 21:7**

Be sober, be vigilant; because your adversary the devil, as a roaring lion, walketh about, seeking whom he may devour: **1 Peter 5:8**

The entire nation suffered as a result of David's mistake. We must be watchful and alert as we sit on the throne of David. The New English Bible translation says, *"Awake! Be on the alert."* We cannot be asleep as we sit on the throne of David. We cannot be ignorant of Satan's devices.

This is one of the few times Satan is named in the Old Testament. He is mentioned in connection with David. He was working behind the scenes to get David into a position where God's judgment would fall. Satan is always trying to tempt us as we sit on David's throne. He hates and fears the throne of David. He does not want us to rule and reign on this throne.

Wherefore we would have come unto you, even I Paul, once and again; but Satan hindered us.
1 Thessalonians 2:18

And the God of peace shall bruise Satan under your feet shortly....
Romans 16:20

And he said unto them, I beheld Satan as lightning fall from heaven.
Luke 10:18

Satan will attempt to hinder us as we sit on David's throne, but God will bruise him under our feet. Other translations say, *"shall crush Satan under your feet."* We have power to tread on serpents and scorpions. We will see Satan crushed under our feet as we sit on the throne of David. Exercise your authority over Satan as you sit on the throne of David.

Chapter 14
Ruling and Reigning with Jesus on the Throne of David

Ruling and Reigning From Zion

There are many Scriptures concerning Zion that are prophetic concerning the end-time Church. I encourage every believer to meditate upon these Scriptures. Allow them to sink deep into your spirit. A revelation of Zion will change your life and ministry causing you to enjoy the benefits of dominion and prosperity.

> **Nevertheless David took the stronghold of Zion: the same is the city of David.**
> **2 Samuel 5:7**

> **And David dwelt in the castle; therefore they called it the city of David.**
>
> **So David waxed greater and greater: for the LORD of hosts was with him.**
> **1 Chronicles 11:7,9**

> **But ye are come unto mount Sion, and unto the city of the living God, the heavenly Jerusalem, and to an innumerable company of angels.**
> **Hebrews 12:22**

David took the stronghold of Zion which became the city of David. This was a significant victory for

David. Zion was a fortress. David waxed greater and greater after this victory.

David ruled from Zion. We are connected to the heavenly Zion through Jesus Christ. Zion is the city of the king. There is an innumerable company of angels connected to Zion. Zion churches will experience the ministry of angels in deliverance, healing, financial breakthroughs and supernatural protection. These churches are end-time, Davidic churches. Warring angels will fight for them and assist them in carrying out their commissions.

The crown is fallen from our head: woe unto us that we have sinned!

Because of the mountain of Zion, which is desolate, the foxes walk upon it.

Turn thou us unto thee, O LORD, and we shall be turned; renew our days as of old.
Lamentations 5:16,18,21

Zion became desolate. The tabernacle of David fell down. This is the message of the Lamentations of Jeremiah. He wept over Zion. Jesus wept over Jerusalem.

God is in the process of restoring Zion. We are living in *days of restoration*. The Church is Zion. The city of David and the tabernacle of David is being rebuilt by Jesus the Greater David. Jeremiah saw the destruction of Zion. We are living to see the restoration of Zion. Jeremiah wept. We rejoice.

The crown that was fallen has been placed upon the head of Jesus the Greater David (Revelation 14:14). Jesus inherits the crown of His father David. He rules and reigns from Zion. We rule with Him through this crown. We are living to see the crown of David restored to Zion. Begin to see yourself wearing this crown. You are a king and a priest. Who ever heard of a king without a crown? The high priest also had a crown (Exodus 29:6).

A crown represents power and authority. We have inherited a crown of glory through Jesus Christ. The crown of David will flourish (Psalms 132:18). God's kingdom is always expanding. Our authority is increasing. We are operating in more and more authority each year. Of the increase of His government there shall be no end (Isaiah 9:7).

Yet have I set my king upon my holy hill of Zion.

I will declare the decree: the LORD hath said unto me, Thou art my Son; this day have I begotten thee.

Ask of me, and I shall give thee the heathen for thine inheritance, and the uttermost parts of the earth for thy possession.
Psalm 2:6-8

Jesus, the Greater David, rules from Zion. We rule with Him on the throne of David. We can ask for the nations. We can possess the uttermost parts of the earth. This is the authority of Zion believers and Zion churches.

God dwells in Zion. Zion churches are filled with the presence and glory of God. God shines out of Zion. There is rejoicing in Zion! *(Psalms 9:11; Psalms 48:1; Psalms 50:2; Psalms 76:2)*

And of Zion it shall be said, This and that man was born in her....
Psalm 87:5

It is a blessing to be born in Zion! Many of us have been birthed in this new move of God. Those born in Zion are birthed in strength. They come forth with a spirit of David. We have been birthed in the apostolic and prophetic move. There are certain characteristics of those born in Zion. They are birthed in praise, worship, and rejoicing. They are birthed in the presence and glory of God. They are birthed in intercession and warfare.

Thou shalt arise, and have mercy upon Zion: for the time to favour her, yea, the set time has come.

Psalm 102:13

Zion was prophetic of the Church. We are Zion. Jesus dwells in Zion, the Church. God is having mercy upon Zion. This is the set time of God's favor. Begin to see a new level of favor operating in your life. You are a part of Zion. All these Scriptures on Zion are prophetic of the end-time Church. We rule and reign from Zion.

When the LORD shall build up Zion, he shall appear in his glory.

Psalm 102:16

Get ready to experience new levels of glory! God is building up His church. He has promised to appear in His glory. We are experiencing the manifest presence of God. Jesus sits on a throne of glory. We reign from a throne of glory. The glory of God rests upon your life. You are a Zion believer. Begin to see yourself ministering in His glory.

Let them be confounded and turned back that hate Zion.

Psalm 129:5

Those that hate Zion will be confounded and turned back. You cannot hate Zion and prosper. It is the city of the King. The Lord rules out of Zion. His rule is coming through His church and His power is being released through His church. Those that hate you will be confused. You are connected to Zion.

The LORD shall reign forever, even thy God, O Zion, unto all generations. Praise ye the LORD.

Psalm 146:10

Every generation is affected by Zion. Zion churches are governmental, apostolic, ruling churches. They rule through prayer and intercession. They rule through praise and their declarations. God reigns through Zion. Davidic churches are Zion churches. Zion churches have the spirit of David. Zion was the city of David. His throne was in Zion. The throne of David is in the heavenly Zion. We are sitting in heavenly places in Christ.

And it shall come to pass in the last days, that the mountain of the LORD'S house shall be established in the top of the mountains, and shall be exalted above the hills; and all nations shall flow unto it.

And many people shall go and say, Come ye, and let us go up to the mountain of the LORD, to the house of the God of Jacob; and he will teach us his ways, and we will walk in his paths: for out of Zion shall go forth the law, and the word of the LORD from Jerusalem.
Isaiah 2:2,3

This is a prophecy concerning the last-day Church. All nations shall come to Zion. Teaching shall be a characteristic of Zion. God is exalting His house. He is raising up His church. Begin to see all kinds of people coming to you for ministry. Do not limit yourself to one people group. We are seeing all nations come to our churches to be taught the Word of the Lord.

THEREFORE thus saith the Lord GOD, Behold, I lay in Zion for a foundation a stone, a tried stone, a precious corner stone, a sure foundation; he that believeth shall not make haste.
Isaiah 28:16

Jesus is the foundation of Zion. He is the tried stone. He is the precious cornerstone. He is the sure foundation. Zion cannot be moved. It is everlasting. Foundations also speak of apostolic and prophetic ministries. The Church is built upon the foundation of the apostles and prophets, Jesus himself being the chief cornerstone (Ephesians 2:20). Zion churches are built with apostolic and prophetic anointings. They are strong because they have a strong foundation. Zion believers are strong believers. You are a part of Zion through Jesus Christ. You rule and reign from a strong city.

>...so shall the LORD of hosts come down to fight for mount Zion, and for the hill thereof.

>As birds flying, so will the LORD of hosts defend Jerusalem; defending also he will deliver it; and passing over he will preserve it.
>
>**Isaiah 31:4,5**

This is God's word to Zion. He will fight for Zion. He will defend and preserve it. He will deliver Zion. Zion churches are protected by the King. You cannot defeat Zion. Remember there is an innumerable company of angels connected to Zion. We have angelic help and assistance as we rule and reign from Zion.

>AWAKE, awake; put on thy strength, O Zion; put on thy beautiful garments, O Jerusalem, the holy city: for henceforth there shall no more come into thee the uncircumcised and the unclean.
>
>Shake thyself from the dust; arise, and sit down, O Jerusalem: loose thyself from the bands of thy neck, O captive daughter of Zion.
>
>**Isaiah 52:1,2**

It is time for Zion to awake. God is awakening us. We are no longer asleep. We are putting on strength. No more shall unclean spirits come into us. We are loosing ourselves from the bands of the neck. Great deliverance has come to Zion. God has turned our captivity. He has redeemed us from the hand of our enemies. We are arising and sitting on the throne of David.

> The sons also of them that afflicted thee shall come bending unto thee; and all they that despised thee shall bow down at the soles of thy feet; and they shall call thee, The city of the LORD, The Zion of the Holy One of Israel.
>
> Whereas thou hast been forsaken and hated, so that no man went through thee, I will make thee an eternal excellency, a joy of many generations.
>
> Thou shalt also suck the milk of the Gentiles, and shalt suck the breast of kings: and thou shalt know that I the LORD am thy Savior and thy Redeemer, the mighty One of Jacob.
>
> For brass I will bring gold, and for iron I will bring silver, and for wood brass, and for stones iron:...
>
> Isaiah 60:14-17

These are powerful prophetic words concerning Zion. Although you have been despised and hated, God will cause men to bow before you. Great wealth is coming to Zion. God is upgrading us in our finances. You will no longer feel desolate and forsaken. The LORD is our Savior and Redeemer.

> Who hath heard such a thing? who hath seen such things? Shall the earth be made to bring forth in one day? or shall a nation be born at once? for as soon as Zion travailed she brought forth her children.
>
> Isaiah 66:8

Get ready to hear and see things you have never seen before. Nations shall be born at once. Entire people groups shall be swept into the Kingdom when Zion travails. Multitudes shall be born into the Kingdom suddenly. More will be saved in a day than in the previous hundred years. This is the day of great revival! Zion churches are being raised up throughout the earth.

> BUT upon mount Zion shall be deliverance, and there shall be holiness; and the house of Jacob shall possess their possessions.
>
> **Obadiah 1:17**

This is one of my favorite verses of Scripture. I preached from this verse for several months in the church. There is deliverance in Zion. Zion believers cast out demons. They bring deliverance to nations. This is a part of ruling and reigning on the throne of David.

Holiness is a part of Zion. We are to worship God in the beauty of holiness. Zion is a holy city. God's throne is built on holiness. Holiness is our strength. We are a holy people. Zion is connected to holy angels. Our God is a Holy God. His Name is Holy. Commit yourself to a lifestyle of holiness. Let holiness be the characteristic of your life and ministry.

The house of Jacob shall possess their possessions on Mount Zion. Get ready to receive your inheritance. Get ready to possess your possessions. Your possessions are on Mount Zion. Your inheritance is in Zion. It is the city of the King. We are born in Zion. We live in Zion. We experience the blessings of Zion.

> Arise and thresh, O daughter of Zion: for I will make thine horn iron, and I will make thine hoofs brass: and thou shalt beat in pieces many people: and I will consecrate their gain unto the LORD, and their substance unto the Lord of the whole earth.
>
> **Micah 4:13**

It is time to arise and thresh. To *thresh* means to trample, tear, tread down. This is what Zion churches and believers will do to the powers of darkness. This includes the nations. Their gain will be consecrated to the LORD. There is much financial release and wealth transfer when we thresh and beat down the powers of hell. Remember great wealth is connected to David's throne. Zion is the city of David. We are connected to the heavenly Zion through Jesus the greater David. We rule and reign with him from Zion.

> **SING and rejoice, O daughter of Zion: for lo, I come, and I will dwell in the midst of thee, saith the LORD.**
>
> **And many nations shall be joined to the LORD in that day, and shall be my people: and I will dwell in the midst of thee, and thou shalt know that the LORD of hosts hath sent me unto thee.**
> **Zechariah 2:10,11**

Zion is a place of singing and rejoicing. This is a sign of a Zion church. God dwells in Zion. This is the manifest presence of God. Many nations are joined to the Lord because of Zion. Many nations are coming to your ministry. They are attracted to Zion. David prophesied and sang about the nations. His desire was to see the nations worship the God of Israel. This was the heart of David. It will also be the heart of Zion.

The prophets were prophesying about the last days. They were prophesying about us. You are the result of these prophetic utterances. You have come into the Kingdom for such a time as this. You are not here by accident. This is a part of your destiny. Begin to see yourself through the eyes of prophecy. Allow these prophecies to bring you forth into your purpose and destiny. War with these prophecies. Confess them and believe them. You will begin to see the course of your life change.

> **In that day it shall be said to Jerusalem, Fear thou not: and to Zion, Let not thine hands be slack.**
>
> **The LORD thy God in the midst of thee is mighty; he will save, he will rejoice over thee with joy; he will rest in his love, he will joy over thee with singing.**
> **Zephaniah 3:16**

God is in the midst of Zion! He is mighty to save. There is much salvation in Zion. Salvation is healing, deliverance, wholeness, and protection. God rejoices over Zion! He sings over Zion. We have experienced this many times in our services through the song of the LORD. Begin to see God rejoicing over you. He takes pleasure in His people. God sings over you. You can rule and reign from Zion with King Jesus. Zion churches are ruling churches. They exercise authority over principalities and powers. They are apostolic, governmental, territorial, ruling churches.

As New Testament believers we have access to the blessings of mercy, deliverance, favor, fame, wealth, provision, wisdom, revelation, authority, power, dominion, and victory as we sit upon the throne of David. Allow these truths to be firmly established in your heart. Meditate upon these truths. Confess them daily. You will begin to see the manifestation of these truths in your own life. We are seated in heavenly places in Christ. As we walk in obedience, humility, and faith we will walk in new levels of power and authority. We experience a new anointing for breakthrough and dominion. Rise up, dear believer, and take your place on the throne of David!